WORLD SPEEDWAY FINAL

A history from 1929

by Maurice Jones

with additional chapters by Mike Nicks and Peter Oakes

Macdonald and Jane's Publishers Ltd

Published by Macdonald & Jane's Publishers Ltd, Paulton
House, 8 Shepherdess Walk, London N1 7LW in association
with EMAP National Publications Ltd,
21 Church Walk, Peterborough PE1 2TW.

Set and composed by the CALL Printing Group,
Cambridge and St. Ives.
Colour process by Woolthame Ltd, London EC3.
Printed in Great Britain by Hazell Watson and Viney Ltd.,
Aylesbury, Bucks.

ISBN 0 354 08551 4

8001

Contents

The following key should be used in conjunction with the score tables and heat-by-heat charts that accompany reports of finals from 1935-38 and from 1949-78:

ns —————————— non-starter
ef —————————— engine failure
exc —————————— excluded
f —————————— fell
f/exc or f/e ——— fell, excluded
f/re or f/r ——— fell, remounted
ret —————————— retired
dns —————————— did not start
nf —————————— non-finisher

Photographic contributors include Brian Holder, Trevor Meeks, Mike Patrick, Alf Weedon and Wright Wood, *Motor Cycle News* also provided many of the pictures.

Front cover picture: Ole Olsen under the floodlights at Wembley in 1975.
Back cover: Vic Huxley, a leading contender in pre-war championship events.
Pages 2-3: Ray Tauser, winner of the 1931 *Star* final. Pages 150-151: from left, Marek Cieslak, Jan Verner, and Scott Autrey in the 1978 world final.

Introduction

FOR ANY SPEEDWAY follower, the World Championship Final is *the* meeting of the year to attend. It may not always provide the most thrilling racing, and injuries and other circumstances often prevent a full quota of the world's top riders from qualifying for the final. But undoubtedly, the event is guaranteed to ensure the biggest crowd of the year, and the ultimate in highly charged emotion. Speedway history tells us that the first ever world final took place at Wembley on 10 September 1936, and that the first world champion was Australian Lionel Van Praag. However, long before that significant date in London many other meetings had been dubbed 'world championship', although none of the contests — which took place at venues as far apart as Paris and Sydney — ever received official blessing.

The true fore-runners of the world finals were in fact the *Star* championships held in Britain between 1929 and 1935. Sponsored by the London evening *Star* newspaper, these events were not truly representative of the best in international speedway at that time, particularly in their early stages. Due to their importance in the evolution of the world championship, however, details of these meetings are included in this book. The introduction of a genuine world championship in 1936 started with a controversy. The argument centred around the addition on world final night of bonus points riders had scored in qualifying rounds. Illustrating the pitfalls in this system, 'Bluey' Wilkinson won all his races in the final, yet finished only third overall. Two other riders, winner Van Praag and runner-up Eric Langton, had scored more bonus points in their qualifying rounds, and thus were credited with higher finishing positions than the luckless Wilkinson. The outbreak of World War Two just four days before the scheduled 1939 world final caused it to be cancelled. With the resumption of civilian life after the war speedway returned with a bang, and was presented in front of huge crowds. But the world final itself was not staged immediately. Instead, the British Riders' Championship, open to the best available talent at that time, was run for three years. As these events repre-sented the most important international speedway gatherings of their day, full

by Maurice Jones

details of them are included here, together with a list of qualifiers for the ill-fated 1939 world final. The return of the world final proper in 1949 was an incredible event, with tickets being as hard to purchase as soccer Cup Final tickets. The racing was held on a Thursday, and the first post-war champion was England's Tommy Price. At 38 years of age, this was a magnificent performance. In the fifties speedway entered a period of the doldrums, with many tracks closing down. So, to combat the rivalry of television, the world final was switched to a Saturday night in 1956. By now the world final was fully representative of the best talent in speedway, and gradually riders from the Continent began to make their presence felt. Swedish riders were particularly successful, and inevitably there were demands that the world final should not be raced perennially at Wembley. The first occasion that the final was run outside London was in 1961, the venue being Malmo in Sweden. Since that time finals have also been staged at Gothenburg in Sweden, and at Wroclaw and Katowice in Poland. Subsequently, Australia, Russia, and the USA have made approaches to hold the event, and Denmark may well have a legitimate claim in the near future. Of the finalists themselves, 216 riders have contested 33 finals to date, and they have represented 17 nations. Ove Fundin and Ivan Mauger have each won five finals, and Barry Briggs has taken four. Between them, these three great riders have competed in a total of 46 finals, scored no less than 536 points, and have won 133 individual races on the big nights. Complete statistical details of every rider's and nation's performances can be found in this book, together with many rare photographs of early contestants, and several other feature sections that I hope will add up to a memorable and even historic book for the dedicated speedway follower. Many hours of research have been spent in compiling this book, and I would like to acknowledge the assistance given to me by my friends Dave Welch and Mike Holt, who loaned material that helped to confirm my own sources of information. I would also like to thank George Greenwood, Jack Parker, Tommy Price, and Freddie Williams, who provided some of the pictures used.

Typical action from the *Star* championship era, as Phil Bishop leads Roger Frogley, the winner of the English section of the 1929 final.

The 'Star' Championship 1929-35

The origins of the World Speedway Championship can be traced back half a century to a knock-out competition held on various tracks in England in 1929. But six years later the *Star* championship had evolved into a formula that set the pattern for future world finals.

1929-34
'Star' Championship

WITH THE ARRIVAL of league racing in Britain in 1929 it was obvious that before long there would be arguments as to who was the best rider of the day. At that time promoters were divided into northern and southern regions. The southerners formed themselves into an organisation verbosely entitled the Association of Motor Cycle Track Racing Promoters, and decided to run an individual championship with the aim of deciding the world's ultimate speedway rider. It was considered that the overseas riders from America and Australia were too good for their British counterparts, and the competition was therefore split into two sections, Overseas and Home. Sponsorship was arranged from the London *Star* newspaper, and the

Dropped handlebars, inside leg trailing — Ray Tauser, the 1931 *Star* final winner, displays the vivid style

championship was born. It was known as the *Star* Riders Trophy.

The competition was run on similar lines to today's Golden Helmet series. Selected riders met in pairs and competed over three races during two occasions in a season when their respective teams met on a home and away basis. The very first of these confrontations took place at Southampton in June 1929 between Billy Galloway and 'Sprouts' Elder. After all the eliminating contests had been held the finalists emerged as Australians Vic Huxley and Frank Arthur in the Overseas section, and Roger Frogley and Jack Parker in the Home division. Arthur and Frogley raced on to become the first *Star* champions.

The competition resumed in 1930 with one major difference — British riders were now considered good enough to compete on equal terms with the foreigners. Another modification to the event was that the home and away eliminating races were scrapped, to be replaced by a grand final at Wembley. The contestants were the top 12 scorers from the first 15 league matches of the season. Three riders at a time lined up in eliminating races, and eventually the only two Australian riders present won through to the final. These were in fact the same pair, Vic Huxley and Frank Arthur, who had ridden through to the Overseas final in the previous year, but this time there was a reversal of the result, and Huxley emerged as the winner.

Frank Arthur (above) and Roger Frogley (below) were the Overseas and Home winners of the historic 1929 *Star* championship, from which the world finals evolved.

typical of the period.

In 1931 each track held its own eliminating round to decide which riders would go through to the Wembley final — the previous year's system of selecting the league's top scorers had not proved popular with the fans. Jack Parker was the 1931 favourite but for the first time an American, Ray Tauser, raced in the event — and won it. In the crucial race Parker was badly bunched in on the first turn and Tauser and Vic Huxley battled it out, with the American leading all the way. Tommy Croombs was third, Parker being disqualified for crossing the track's inner white line.

The following season saw another major change in the organisation of the competition. The Association of Motor Cycle Track Racing Promoters was disbanded and an amalgamation of tracks in the north and south appeared under the title of the National Speedway Association. To mark the debut of the northern aces, the event too was given a new name, the *Star* National Speedway Championship. The competition itself was run on the lines of the previous year, and the final saw the great Eric Langton become the first Englishman to win the title. The persistent Huxley was second, and his Australian team-mate from the Wimbledon track, Dicky Case, was third.

In 1933 the championship's qualifying formula was changed to allow two members from each legue team to compete at Wembley. This final produced some of the finest speedway ever seen, and was won by one of England's greatest ever riders, Tom Farndon. His Australian partner at the Crystal Palace venue, Ron Johnson, was runner-up, and the red-headed 'Bluey' Wilkinson a gallant third. What of the usually ever-

Above left: Ron Johnson, second in the 1933 event, falls after tangling with the rear wheel of another contestant.

Left: From left, Norman Parker, 1933 *Star* winner Tom Farndon, Al Wilkinson and Stan Greatrex. Below: Australian Max Grosskreutz was among competitors in the 1929 *Star* championship. .

present Vic Huxley? For the first time since the institution of the competition in 1929 he failed to make the top two placings.

Injury prevented the consistent Huxley from even qualifying for the 1934 *Star* Championship. In his absence the 1932 winner Eric Langton, the 1929 finalist Jack Parker, and the popular Wembley rider Ginger Lees won through to the final race. Langton was the hot favourite but the brilliant Parker had other ideas and proceeded to take a popular victory by passing Langton from the back, a tactic that was rare in those days.

1929 *Star* Championship
Overseas Section:
Winner: Frank Arthur (Australia) from Vic Huxley (Australia)

Other qualifiers: Stan Catlett (Australia), Sprouts Elder (USA), Max Grosskreutz (Australia), Alf Chick (Australia), Billy Galloway (Australia), Billy Lamont (Australia), Art Pechar (USA), Ron Johnson (Australia)

English Section:
Roger Frogley beat Jack Parker

Other qualifiers: Jim Kempster, Buster Frogley, Ivor Creek, Tommy Croombs, Jimmy Hayes, Colin Watson, Eric Spencer, Gus Kuhn

1930 *Star* Final
Winner: Vic Huxley (Australia) from Frank Arthur (Australia)

Other qualifiers: Jack Ormston (England), Roger Frogley (England), Colin Watson (England), +George Taylor (England), Harry Taft (England), Tiger Stevenson (England), Tom Farndon (England), Jim Kempster (England), Squibb Burton (England), Sid Jackson (England)

+George Taylor took the place of Triss Sharp, who had qualified for the final but was injured prior to the event.

1931 *Star* Final
Winner: Ray Tauser (USA)
Second: Vic Huxley (Australia)
Third: Tommy Croombs (England)

Other qualifiers: Jack Parker (England), Colin Watson (England), Harry Shepherd (England), Sid Edmonds (England), Phil Bishop (England), Sid Jackson (England), Les Patrick (England), Ernie Rickman (England), Arthur Warwick (England), Fred Strecker (England), Norman Kendrick (England), Colin Stewart (Australia), Bluey Wilkinson (Australia), Charlie Spinks (Australia), Harold Hastings (Australia), Ron Johnson (Australia), Frank Arthur (Australia), Squibb Burton (England), Billy Ellmore (England)

1932 *Star* Final
Winner: Eric Langton (England)
Second: Vic Huxley (Australia)
Third: Dicky Case (Australia)

Other qualifiers: Frank Varey (England), Jack Parker (England), Norman Parker (England), Roy Dook (England), Sid Jackson (England), Bill Clibbett (England), Gordon Byers (England), Ginger Lees (England), Les Wotton (England), Tommy Croombs (England), Wal Phillips (England), Tom Farndon (England), Bert Spencer (Australia), Frank Arthur (Australia), Ron Johnson (Australia), Joe Francis (England), Eric Collins (England)

1933 *Star* Final
Winner: Tom Farndon (England)
Second: Ron Johnston (Australia)
Third: Bluey Wilkinson (Australia)

Other qualifiers: Norman Parker (England), Phil Bishop (England), Eric Langton (England), Frank Varey (England), Colin Watson (England), Harry Whitfield (England), Tommy Croombs (England), Les Wotton (England), Stan Greatrex (England), Colin Moore (England), Eddie Blain (England), Sid Jackson (England), Frank Goulden (England), Vic Huxley (Australia), Jack Sharp (Australia), Dicky Case (Australia), Jack Chapman (Australia)

1934 *Star* Final
Winner: Jack Parker (England)
Second: Eric Langton (England)
Third: Ginger Lees (England)

Other qualifiers: Bob Harrison (England), Colin Watson (England), Claude Rye (England), Sid Jackson (England), Tommy Croombs (England), Dusty Haigh (England), Les Wotton (England), George Newton (England), Bluey Wilkinson (Australia), Dicky Case (Australia), Ron Johnson (Australia), Jack Chapman (Australia), Jack Sharp (Australia), Mick Murphy (Australia), *Joe Francis (England)

*indicates injured, unable to ride in final.

1935 'Star' Championship

THIS YEAR was to see the last of the *Star*-sponsored championships which had been a highlight of the previous six seasons. The entire structure of the competition was also changed from the qualifying rounds to the final itself. This season each track staged a qualifying round, and at Wembley the final was raced over 20 heats with the 16 riders meeting each other once. Another modification was the introduction of four-man races, replacing the three-man heats used in the finals of previous years.

The largest crowd of the season was disappointed to hear that two of the more fancied riders, Tom Farndon and Ron Johnson, had been badly hurt in a crash at New Cross the previous evening. In fact Farndon was in a critical condition at the time the final was being raced off, and was to die the day after. The atmosphere of the meeting was marred by news of this accident, but reserves Geoff Pymar and Norman Parker were brought in to replace the injured men. Bob Harrison of Belle Vue was in fact scheduled as second reserve, but was unable to reach the stadium.

Frank Charles, who had come out of retirement earlier in the season to join the Wembley Lions, won the final with a maximum points score. As pointers to

Vic Huxley's stylish riding was a feature of the 1935 final.

his form, a month or so before the big occasion he had won both the Gold Cup and the Wembley qualifying round of the championship. In the final itself he was never seriously challenged except by Eric Langton in heat 17, when the latter led for two laps before being passed.

The highlight of the meeting occurred in heat 14, which brought together three riders unbeaten at that point, Charles, Max Grosskreutz and Jack Ormston. It was obviously to be a crucial race, and opened with Ormston being crowded on the first turn, an incident that left him little chance of making up lost ground. In the meantime Grosskreutz had taken the lead, with Charles pressing him from two lengths behind. On the third lap Grosskreutz succumbed to the pressure, overslid and fell. Charles and Ormston both did well to avoid the fallen rider. Charles raced on to win from Ormston, while Grosskreutz was able to remount and take third place, as Bill Kitchen had already retired from the race.

Score Chart

								Total
1 Frank Charles	England	3	3	3	3	3	15
2 Jack Ormston	England	3	3	3	2	3	14
3 Max Grosskreutz	Australia	3	3	3	1	3	13
4 Eric Langton	England	0	3	2	3	2	10
Bluey Wilkinson	Australia	2	2	3	1	2	10
Jack Parker	England	2	2	0	3	3	10
7 Vic Huxley	Australia	3	1	1	2	2	9
8 Dicky Case	Australia	1	2	2	3	nf	8
9 Tommy Croombs	England	2	1	2	1	1	7
10 Norman Parker (res)	England	2	1	1	2	0	6
11 Bill Kitchen	England	1	2	1	0	nf	4
Tiger Stevenson	England	0	0	2	1	1	4
13 Geoff Pymar (res)	England	1	1	0	0	1	3
Lionel Van Praag	Australia	1	0	2	0	0	3
15 Jack Sharp	Australia	0	0	1	0	nf	1
16 Wally Kilmister	New Zealand	f	ns	ns	ns	ns	0
Tom Farndon	England	(unfit due to injuries)					
Ron Johnson	Australia	(unfit due to injuries)					
Bob Harrison (res)	England	(did not ride)					

Heat-by-heat

		Time
1	Grosskreutz, Wilkinson, Case, Langton	76.2s
2	Charles, Parker, Van Praag, Sharp	76.2s
3	Ormston, Croombs, Pymar, Kilmister (f)	77.8s
4	Huxley, Parker, Kitchen, Stevenson	77.0s
5	Langton, Kitchen, Pymar, Van Praag	78.8s
6	Grosskreutz, Parker, Croombs, Stevenson	77.8s
7	Ormston, Case, Parker, Sharp	77.8s
8	Charles, Wilkinson, Huxley, Kilmister (ns)	76.4s
9	Ormston, Langton, Huxley, Parker	77.8s
10	Grosskreutz, Van Praag, Parker, Kilmister (ns)	78.6s
11	Langton, Stevenson, Sharp, Kilmister (ns)	78.8s
12	Wilkinson, Croombs, Kitchen, Sharp	78.6s
13	Case, Stevenson, Pymar	77.8s
14	Charles, Ormston, Grosskreutz (f/re), Kitchen (nf)	78.8s
15	Case, Huxley, Croombs, Van Praag	79.8s
16	J Parker, N Parker, Wilkinson, Pymar	78.6s
17	Charles, Langton, Croombs, N Parker	79.6s
18	Grosskreutz, Huxley, Pymar, Sharp	80.4s
19	Parker, Case (nf), Kitchen (nf), Kilmister (ns)	79.8s
20	Ormston, Wilkinson, Stevenson, Van Praag	80.0s

Jack Ormston was the surprise package of the night and scored a well deserved 14 points to take runner-up position. He toyed with the more fancied Jack Parker, Eric Langton and Dicky Case, and might well have emerged as overall winner if he had not been baulked in that all-important heat 14. The same could be said for Grosskreutz's error of judgement when he fell in the same race. Grosskreutz and Charles created a new joint track record in heats one and two, while Charles equalled the old track record as late in the meeting as heat eight.

Langton, Kitchen, Dicky Case, Bluey Wilkinson and Vic Huxley were all disappointing on the night, giving only rare glimpses of their usual form. Of these riders Huxley was the most successful, his 10-point score including a spectacular win in heat four when he took all three of his opponents from the back.

Wembley's New Zealander Wally Kilmister was injured in an early fall and took no further part in the meeting, while Jack Parker drew generous applause in heat 19 for skillfully laying down his machine to avoid the fallen Dicky Case. Another feature of the meeting was the plucky riding of Parker's younger brother Norman, who scored six points from the reserve position.

Wembley supporters were delighted that one of their own riders, Charles, had won a national championship at the stadium for the first time. But many spectators wondered what might have been if Farndon had not suffered his fatal accident the previous evening. Until that point in the season his riding record had been unequalled, and at that time he was without doubt the finest rider in the world.

Frank Charles won the last of the *Star* finals with an unbeaten score.

Main picture: A battle between two pre-war finalists, as Vic Huxley rides outside Jack Parker. Insets, from left: the first World Speedway Champion, Lionel Van Praag; Wilbur Lamoreaux, second in 1937; 1937 champion Jack Milne is greeted by England's Bill Kitchen (standing); and the legendary 1938 champion, Bluey Wilkinson.

The World Championship 1936-39

Dominated by Australian and American riders in these pioneering years, the world final rapidly developed into such a popular contest that the last event to be held before the war filled Wembley stadium with a capacity crowd of 93,000.

1936
Van Praag
—first world
champion

THE FIRST OFFICIAL World Speedway Championship was staged at Wembley on 10 September 1936. And to match the event's new title, it had matured into a truly international contest, with riders having to fight through an initial qualifying round and then a championship round in order to reach the Wembley final.

Sixty-three riders entered the qualifying rounds — 36 Britons, 11 Australians, three Americans and three Danes, two men each from Sweden, Germany and Spain, and single representatives from New Zealand, Canada, France, and South Africa. Two Rumanians were also scheduled to ride, but failed to make an appearance. The top 28 scorers from the qualifying rounds reached the championship eliminators, each rider having to enter four of these events, which were spread over the seven league tracks operating that season. The 16 survivors from the championship rounds were made up of nine Englishmen, four Australians and two Americans, only one rider from

Eric Langton, runner-up in speedway's first world final, leads Bluey Wilkinson during an England v Australia test match at Wembley.

Continental Europe winning through, the Dane, Morian Hansen. Jack Parker and Joe Abbott had both qualified, but injury prevented them from competing. Arthur Atkinson replaced Parker while Abbott's replacement, Ron Johnson, was himself injured, and Bill Pitcher was the eventual lucky substitute.

The major talking point of the 1936 final was the controversial way in which bonus points earned in the qualifying rounds were carried forward and added to riders' scores at Wembley. For example, the highest scorer from the qualifiers, Eric Langton, was able to start the evening's racing with 13 bonus points already on his side. Bearing in mind that the winner at Wembley would take away a cash prize of £500 — equivalent to some £6,000 at today's prices — there were justified resentments against the bonus system.

A crowd of 66,000 was privileged to see one of the finest finals yet staged at Wembley. The winner was Australian Lionel Van Praag, who beat Eric Langton by less than a machine's length in a pulsating run-off for the title. Many spectators, however, were more than sympathetic to the cause of Bluey Wilkinson, who won all five of his races, yet lacked sufficient qualifying points to be crowned champion. Wikinson could not even claim the £400 second prize, as his 10 bonus points brought his total score to 25, enough to gain only the £100 third place. Wilkinson had even had to ride heats 13 and 14 back-to-back without a rest. His chief rivals in these two races were Langton and van Praag respectively, yet he defeated both of them and was without doubt the finest rider on the night. Wilkinson's case was to stand as the main argument for the abandonment of the bonus points system at a future date.

One of the more fancied contestants this year was Frank Charles, the *Star* Championship winner in 1935. After wins in his first two races he appeared to be strongly in contention, but he missed the gate in his next ride and managed only two more points from his remaining two outings. American Cordy Milne was best placed of the foreign contingent in joint fourth spot, but Vix Huxley, in what proved to be his only appearance in a world final, failed to win a race. The once great Australian was a mere shadow of the man who had dominated the *Star* championships a few years previously. An injury incurred in a previous meeting was one of his problems, and in fact it forced his retirement from the sport at the end of the 1936 season.

This season saw Wal Phillips, Bill Pitcher, Bob Harrison and Dicky Case make their only apperances in a world final, but perhaps the major point of conjecture in the 1936 event was Eric Langton's breaking of the tapes in his anxiety to get started in the vital run-off against Van Praag. One can only speculate on the outcome of such an action in these days of greater professionalism and tighter rules.

Score Chart

								Total	Bonus	Grand Total
1 Lionel Van Praag	Australia	3	3	3	2	3		14	12	26
2 Eric Langton	England	3	3	3	2	2		13	13	26
3 Bluey Wilkinson	Australia	3	3	3	3	3		15	10	25
4 Cordy Milne	USA	2	2	1	3	3		11	9	20
Frank Charles	England	3	3	0	2	0		8	12	20
6 Dicky Case	Australia	2	0	3	1	2		8	9	17
Jack Ormston	England	1	1	2	3	1		8	9	17
Vic Huxley	Australia	1	2	0	2	2		7	10	17
9 George Newton	England	0	0	3	1	0		4	12	16
10 Jack Milne	USA	1	2	1	0	2		6	9	15
Morian Hansen	Denmark	2	1	2	f	0		5	10	15
Bob Harrison	England	0	0	2	0	3		5	10	15
13 Wal Phillips	England	1	1	0	2	1		5	7	12
14 Ginger Lees	England	2	0	1	0	1		4	7	11
15 Arthur Atkinson	England	0	2	1	0	0		3	6	9
16 Bill Pitcher	England	0	1	exc	exc	1		2	6	8
17 Norman Parker (res)	England					1		1	6	7
Jack Parker	England	(unfit, did not ride)							12	

Heat-by-heat

		Time
1	Charles, Case, Phillips, Newton	73.6s
2	Wilkinson, Lees, Ormston, Atkinson	77.2s
3	Van Praag, C Milne, J Milne, Pitcher	75.8s
4	Langton, Hansen, Huxley, Harrison	76.8s
5	Charles, C Milne, Ormston, Harrison	75.4s
6	Langton, Atkinson, Pitcher, Case	77.4s
7	Van Praag, Huxley, Phillips, Lees	77.6s
8	Wilkinson, J Milne, Hansen, Newton	78.6s
9	Van Praag, Hansen, Atkinson, Charles	76.6s
10	Case, Ormston, J Milne, Huxley	78.6s
11	Langton, Charles, Lees, J Milne	76.8s
12	Newton, Harrison, N Parker, Lees, Pitcher (exc)	77.8s
13	Wilkinson, Langton, C Milne, Phillips	77.2s
14	Wilkinson, Van Praag, Case, Harrison	76.6s
15	Ormston, Phillips, Hansen (f), Pitcher (exc)	79.6s
16	C Milne, Huxley, Newton, Atkinson	78.4s
17	Wilkinson, Huxley, Pitcher, Charles	78.6s
18	C Milne, Case, Lees, Hansen	78.8s
19	Harrison, J Milne, Phillips, Atkinson	79.8s
20	Van Praag, Langton, Ormston, Newton	78.2s
21	Van Praag beat Langton in run-off for 1st place	

Dicky Case (left) scored eight points in the final to add to his nine bonus points. Bill Pitcher gained only two points in the only world final for which he qualified.

1937
Milnes and Lamoreaux make American triple

DESPITE the criticism of the invidious bonus points system that had been aired the previous year, it was retained for 1937. The method of qualifying was modified, however, the number of initial entrants being reduced to 48. Each rider had to compete in two meetings on First Division tracks, and the top 28 scorers then progressed to ride in four further qualifying rounds on National League ovals. The best 16 from these events then went forward to the Wembley final.

The rider most fancied to win on the big night was American Jack Milne, whose performances for New Cross during the season had been nothing short of brilliant. In addition, he headed the qualifiers with 13 bonus points, and the anticipated challenge from Bluey Wilkinson never materialised after the latter had injured a wrist earlier in the season and was unable to qualify.

On the night of the final Wembley entertained its largest speedway crowd to date — no less than 85,000. They watched an American domination when

America's top trio (from left): Wilbur Lamoreaux, Jack Milne, and Cordy Milne.

Jack Milne duly raced to an unbeaten 15-point score, Wilbur Lamoreaux took second place, and Jack's brother Cordy rode into third place. It was indeed a bumper night for the stars and stripes flag, and a popular victory as well, with a large New Cross contingent swelling the thousands of fans.

Two first places followed by a series of mechanical problems saw defending champion Lionel Van Praag finish half-way down the score sheet, while Jack Parker, in fourth place, was the most successful of the English riders. Parker scored consistently in each of his five rides and produced a fine win in heat seven to beat three of his English compatriots. Great things were expected from George Newton who, like Jack Milne, had been having a good season with New Cross. But Newton fell three times, although in the two races he completed he took first and second places. He was joint eighth overall.

Once again, injuries altered the line-up of starters, with West Ham's king of the white line, Tommy Croombs, replacing Bob Harrison. Joe Abbott, who had missed the 1936 final because of injury, made it to Wembley this season but failed to produce his true form, as did his Belle Vue team-mate Bill Kitchen.

Racing on this occasion was again of a high standard, although it was completely dominated by the American trio. Highlights were a fine win by Newton over Cordy Milne in heat two, with the leg-trailing Newton looking in fine form as he beat the Hackney-based American rider in one of the fastest times of the night. Further thrills came in heat four when Van Praag had a great tussle with Arthur Atkinson and won in the fastest time of the night. Ginger Lees performed well on his home league track, beating Kitchen dramatically in heat 18 and finishing in fifth place overall.

Frank Charles, the 1935 *Star* champion, started in disastrous fashion with two non-scoring rides, but hit back to win his two final races, finishing a respectable points total. Speedway's original Great Dane, Morian Hansen, was able to win only one race and was generally disappointing, as was the previous year's runner-up, Eric Langton. Only a win in heat 14 restored a little of Langton's prestige.

One wonders if the red-haired whirlwind from West Ham, Bluey Wilkinson, would have significantly affected the results if he had been riding. However, Wilkinson was certainly up to the task of competing with the big guns from America in the 1938 final . . .

Score Chart

								Total	Bonus	Grand Total
1 Jack Milne	USA	3	3	3	3	3		15	13	28
2 Wilbur Lamoreaux	USA	3	3	3	1	3		13	12	25
3 Cordy Milne	USA	2	3	2	3	2		12	11	23
4 Jack Parker	England	2	3	1	2	2		10	11	21
5 Ginger Lees	England	1	1	2	2	3		9	10	19
6 Frank Charles	England	0	0	1	3	3		7	10	17
Lionel Van Praag	Australia	3	nf	ns	3	0		6	11	17
8 Bill Kitchen	England	1	2	2	2	2		9	7	16
Eric Langton	England	1	nf	0	3	0		4	12	16
George Newton	England	3	f	f	f	2		5	11	16
11 Eric Chitty	Canada	0	2	0	1	1		4	11	15
Morian Hansen	Denmark	1	2	3	1	1		8	7	15
13 Joe Abbott	England	2	1	1	2	0		6	8	14
Arthur Atkinson	England	2	0	2	1	1		6	8	14
15 Frank Varey	England	0	1	1	0	1		3	8	11
16 Tommy Croombs	England	0	2	0	0	0		2	—	2
Alec Statham (res)	England							0		
Ron Johnson (res)	Australia	(did not ride)								

Heat-by-heat

		Time
1	J Milne, Abbott, Langton, Varey	78.2s
2	Newton, C Milne, Kitchen, Charles	77.4s
3	Lamoreaux, Parker, Lees, Croombs	77.8s
4	Van Praag, Atkinson, Hansen, Chitty	77.0s
5	J Milne, Hansen, Lees, Charles	78.2s
6	C Milne, Croombs, Van Praag (nf), Langton (nf)	no time
7	Parker, Kitchen, Abbott, Atkinson	77.8s
8	Lamoreaux, Chitty, Varey, Newton (f)	77.4s
9	J Milne, C Milne, Parker, Chitty	78.0s
10	Lamoreaux, Atkinson, Charles, Langton	78.2s
11	J Milne, Kitchen, Lamoreaux, Statham, Van Pragg (ns)	78.0s
12	Hansen, Kitchen, Varey, Croombs	78.8s
13	Van Praag, Lees, Abbott, Newton (f)	76.8s
14	Langton, Parker, Hansen, Newton (f)	78.4s
15	Charles, Abbott, Chitty, Croombs	78.8s
16	C Milne, Lees, Atkinson, Varey	79.4s
17	J Milne, Newton, Atkinson, Croombs	78.8s
18	Lees, Kitchen, Chitty, Langton	78.8s
19	Lamoreaux, C Milne, Hansen, Abbott	78.4s
20	Charles, Parker, Varey, Van Praag	78.8s

From left, Joe Abbott, Ginger Lees, and Eric Langton were among the 1937 finalists.

1938
Wilkinson's night of courage

CONTROVERSY over the bonus points system remained with the sport, but at least the effects of the arrangement were modified for the 1938 season. Changes were also made to the qualifying methods, with 56 riders from the Second Division fighting it out in preliminary rounds for the distinction of being one of the top six scorers, who then progressed to the first rounds proper. At these events they were joined by 42 First Division stalwarts, the best 28 of this group going forward to a Championship round. This meeting then whittled competitors down to 16 top scorers to ride in the world final at Wembley on 1 September. Bonus points were calculated only on the Championship round, a practice which reduced the gap between the highest and the lowest scorers of the bonuses.

The rider with the best reason for disliking the bonus system was Bluey Wilkinson. It had cost him the world title in 1936, but this year he was determined not to be denied and amassed no less than 53 qualifying points, which earned him the top bonus of eight points under the somewhat complex system being used this season.

Bluey Wilkinson dropped only one point at Wembley in winning the 1938 final.

As it happened, Wilkinson's bonus score was to prove vital: his great rival Jack Milne had seven, as did Wilbur Lamoreaux, and the title was ultimately to depend once again on these points.

The prospect of a fascinating world final attracted a crowd of 93,000, and the atmosphere was as tense as at any championship meeting previously held at Wembley. However, three of the major contestants were doubtful starters due to injury or illness. But Lionel Van Praag, who had damaged a leg, and Jack Milne, who had been suffering from influenza, rallied and were passed fit to ride. The third man in trouble was none other than Wilkinson, who had crashed the previous evening during the second half races at New Cross. Memories of 1935, when the great Tom Farndon received fatal injuries at New Cross on the night prior to Wembley, must have flooded back to Wilkinson. He had hurt his shoulder so badly in the fall that at first he was unable to move an arm, but Saturday morning saw him at the Tottenham Hotspur football ground for special treatment to get him fit for action at Wembley's night of nights. The treatment worked wonders, and although the little Australian was in severe agony he arrived at the stadium assisted by fellow countrymen Clem Mitchell and Len Stewart. He had to be lifted on to his bike to take every one of his rides.

The pattern of the evening's racing took shape during the first five heats. Van Praag, Lamoreaux and Jack Milne each won his first race. Wilkinson then had to ride in heats four and five — and not only did he win them both, he also recorded the fastest times of the night in doing so. It was clear that heat 19, which would bring together Wilkinson and Milne, would be crucial. however, before that Milne dropped a point to Lamoreaux in heat ten, while 'Lammy' had finished in third place behind Bluey and Van Praag in heat five. Predictably, both Milne and Wilkinson won their fourth races, so they lined up for the fateful 19th heat with Milne just one point behind Wilkinson. The other riders in the race were Jack Parker and Cordy Milne, who had won his second and third heats and was himself quite capable of ruining Bluey's anticipated maximum score.

The huge crowd was tense as the four riders lined up knowing that Wilkinson needed only a second place to be crowned champion — but if Cordy Milne could keep the Australian back while Jack won, a run-off would be required to settle the destination of the title. When the tapes rose Jack Milne streaked into the lead followed by his brother, with Wilkinson in third place and Parker at the rear. Then the crowd rose as Wilkinson rode past Cordy Milne into second place. From that point Wilkinson was content to let Jack Milne win the race, in the knowledge that as long as he held on to second place the world championship would be his. Time and again Cordy Milne tried to repass the battling little Aussie, but to no avail. Wilkinson had ridden the meeting of his life in sheer agony from his injured shoulder to become world champion with that second place in his last ride of the night. His points tally at Wembley was 14, identical to Jack Milne's score, but this time the bonus system had worked in his favour, and he won the title with an overall total of 22 points to Milne's 21. It was ample revenge for his 1936 disappointment, and the two Milne brothers were among the first to congratulate him. Such were the nature of his injuries that Wilkinson remains probably the only world final winner never to have received the traditional fling in the air from other riders.

Of the other contestants, Lamoreaux's winning race in heat 15 was equal to the fastest time of the night, and helped him to third place overall. Van Praag proved he was not a spent force by finishing fourth. Bill Kitchen, in joint fifth place with Cordy Milne, enjoyed his best final to date, while England's super stylist Alec Statham at last got his name on a world final score sheet. Tommy Price made his world final debut, as did American Benny Kaufman, who scored a creditable seven points. George Newton and Frank Varey had a poor night, while reserve Jimmy Gibb failed to get a ride and thus become the second Canadian to appear at Wembley. But Jack Ormston, the other reserve, scored five points from just two rides.

Score Chart

								Total	Bonus	Grand Total
1	Bluey Wilkinson	Australia	3	3	3	3	2	14	8	22
2	Jack Milne	USA	3	3	2	3	3	14	7	21
3	Wilbur Lamoreaux	USA	3	1	3	3	3	13	7	20
4	Lionel Van Praag	Australia	3	2	2	1	3	11	7	18
5	Bill Kitchen	England	2	2	1	2	2	9	6	15
	Cordy Milne	USA	1	3	3	0	1	8	7	15
7	Alec Statham	England	2	3	0	0	3	8	5	13
	Eric Langton	England	1	2	2	3	0	8	5	13
9	Benny Kaufman	USA	2	1	0	2	2	7	5	12
10	Jack Parker	England	2	2	2	0	0	6	4	10
	Arthur Atkinson	England	1	0	2	1	1	5	5	10
12	Tommy Price	England	1	0	1	2	0	4	4	8
	Tommy Croombs	England	0	1	1	1	1	4	4	8
14	Geoff Pymar	England	0	0	1	0	1	2	5	7
	George Newton	England	0	1	0	1	0	2	5	7
16	Frank Varey	England	0	0	0	ns	ns	0	4	4
	Jack Ormston (res)	England						3	2	5 —
	Jimmy Gibb (res)	Canada	(did not ride)							—

Heat-by-heat

		Time
1	Van Praag, Parker, Atkinson, Pymar	76.8s
2	Lamoreaux, Statham, C Milne, Newton	75.0s
3	J Milne, Kaufman, Price, Croombs	77.4s
4	Wilkinson, Kitchen, Langton, Varey	76.0s
5	Wilkinson, Van Praag, Lamoreaux, Price	76.2s
6	C Milne, Langton, Croombs, Pymar	77.8s
7	Statham, Parker, Kaufman, Varey	76.0s
8	J Milne, Kitchen, Newton, Atkinson	77.0s
9	C Milne, Van Praag, Kitchen, Kaufman	77.2s
10	Lamoreaux, J Milne, Pymar, Varey	76.6s
11	J Milne, Langton, Van Praag, Statham	75.8s
12	Wilkinson, Atkinson, Croombs, Statham	78.0s
13	Langton, Parker, Price, Newton	77.6s
14	Wilkinson, Kaufman, Newton, Pymar	77.4s
15	Lamoreaux, Kitchen, Croombs, Parker	76.0s
16	Ormston, Price, Atkinson, C Milne	77.6s
17	Van Praag, Ormston, Croombs, Newton	78.2s
18	Statham, Kitchen, Pymar, Price	76.8s
19	J Milne, Wilkinson, C Milne, Parker	77.4s
20	Lamoreaux, Kaufman, Atkinson, Langton	77.6s

1939

War defeats the qualifiers

THE DECLARATION of World War Two forced the cancellation of the 1939 World Final just four days before it was due to take place at Wembley on Thursday, 7 September. Speedway's annual big night had been eagerly anticipated, as reigning champion Bluey Wilkinson had retired to concentrate on the management side of the sport at Sheffield. This meant that the final would inevitably have produced a new champion.

But the anticipated spectacle was not to take place, as attractions that would have drawn large crowds were banned on the outbreak of hostilities because of the fear of heavy casualties in the event of air raids.

Cordy Milne had led the list of qualifiers, but much fancied for the championship was England's Arthur Atkinson, who was in devastating form for West Ham that season. Aub Lawson and a very young Vic Duggan were carrying Australian hopes on this occasion, while Malcolm Craven was scheduled as reserve in what turned out to be the only occasion he qualified for a world final.

Cordy Milne, a scorer in all three previous finals, was top qualifier in 1939.

A non-riding reserve in 1937, Ron Johnson was again unlucky in 1939.

Eric Chitty was one of only two Canadians to qualify for a world final.

Malcolm Craven was reserve on the only occasion he qualified for a final.

1939 Qualifiers

Cordy Milne	(USA)	8
Bill Kitchen	(England)	7
Wilbur Lamoreaux	(USA)	7
Eric Langton	(England)	7
Jack Milne	(USA)	6
Arthur Atkinson	(England)	6
Vic Duggan	(Australia)	6
Lionel Van Praag	(Australia)	6
Alec Statham	(England)	5
Jack Parker	(England)	5
Benny Kaufman	(USA)	5
Ron Johnson	(Australia)	5
Eric Chitty	(Canada)	5
Frank Varey	(England)	4
Eric Collins	(England)	4
Aub Lawson	(Australia)	4
Malcolm Craven	(England)	(res)
Frank Goulden	(England)	(res)

Eric Langton would have been among the favourites if the 1939 event had been run.

Wilbur Lamoreaux was part of the American challenge for the ill-fated 1939 final.

Alec Statham was one of nine English riders who would have appeared at Wembley.

The British Riders' Championship 1946-48

The aftermath of the war prevented an immediate return to world championship racing in the late forties, but the British Riders' series provided dramatic action for crowds starved of entertainment, and produced a trio of great champions.

The great leg-trailer
George Newton powers
inside Jack Mountford
during a British Riders'
qualifying round at
Fleetwood.

1946-48 British Riders' Championship

IN COMMON with other sports, speedway was revived on a national basis in 1946. But as many pre-war riders were still serving in the armed forces and most Commonwealth and foreign riders had returned home during the war, it was decided to stage an alternative meeting to a world final. With sponsorship from the *Sunday Dispatch*, the British Riders' Championship was organised, with contestants from both the National and Northern leagues each having to fight through six qualifying rounds. The top 16 scorers went to Wembley, and one of these in 1946 came from the Northern League, which was the second division in all but name. Belle Vue's Eric Langton emerged as top

The great Jack Parker leads Bill Kitchen. The pair finished first and second in the 1947 British Riders' event, after Parker had won the run-off heat.

qualifier with 81 points, followed by Ron Johnson on 80 and Malcolm Craven with 74.

At Wembley Tommy Price — who rode for the Wembley Lions in league racing anyway — emerged as winner from his team-mate Bill Kitchen. Jack Parker could have made a challenge for the title if he had not fallen in heat six when he met Price, while a noteworthy performance was Frank Hodgson's eight points — he was the best of the Northern League riders.

With the formation of a Third Division in 1947, qualifying rounds for Wembley were extended to these tracks. But of the 28 Third Division hopefuls who entered these rounds only two — Harwood Pike and Vic Pitcher — moved forward to the next qualifiers on Division Two tracks. At this stage 30 riders from the Second Division joined the Third Division men, with each rider competing in a further four qualifying meetings. The top four from these eliminators — Frank Hodgson, Fred 'Kid' Curtis, Will Lowther and Dick Geary — then had to endure another four qualifying sessions in company with First Division riders. Harringay's super Australian Vic Duggan led these qualifiers, scoring the maximum possible 60 points. His closest rival was Norman Parker with 45, followed by Bill Kitchen and George Wilks on 43.

Tommy Price fires up his JAP in front of huge crowds at Wembley in 1946. He won the British Riders' championship that year.

Bill Gilbert was a Wembley league rider when he scored 10 points in the 1948 final.

Duggan's performances so far appeared to make the British Riders' final a mere formality. His first winning ride seemed to confirm this prediction, but a fantastic effort by Jack Parker in heat eight, when he took Duggan from behind, seemed to disturb the great man. Although Duggan won his next race he fell in his fourth and did not start in his last. This left Parker and Kitchen tying on 14 points, so once again a Wembley run-off for the championship provided some superb tactical speedway, with Parker using his immense track craft to gain the verdict. New Cross's little Australian Bill Longley claimed third place with 13 points.

The formula for the 1948 British Riders' Championship remained similar to the previous year's event, with qualifying rounds on Third and Second Division tracks being followed by further rounds on the First Division ovals. Vic Duggan again headed the qualifiers with 57 points out of a possible 60, and Jack Parker was again second best qualifier on 52 points. American Wilbur Lamoreaux, who had returned to

Vic Duggan scored 14 points to win the title in 1948.

British speedway to help the Wembley Lions, was next with 49 points.

In the final Duggan gained revenge for his previous year's defeat with a spectacular win, dropping only one point, to Alec Statham in heat four. Ron Johnson finished the night in runner-up position, and Statham took third place.

Bill Kitchen, who finished second in 1946 and 1947. He also rode for the Wembley league side.

Alec Statham was a finalist in two of the three British Riders' championships.

1946 British Riders' Final

1	Tommy Price	(England)	15
2	Bill Kitchen	(England)	13
3	Jack Parker	(England)	12
4	Eric Langton	(England)	11
5	Malcolm Craven	(England)	10
	Norman Parker	(England)	10
7	Eric Chitty	(Canada)	9
8*	Frank Hodgson	(England)	8
9	Ron Johnson	(Australia)	7
10*	Bert Spencer	(Australia)	5
	Wally Lloyd	(England)	5
12	Bill Longley	(Australia)	4
*	Jeff Lloyd	(England)	4
14*	Tommy Allott	(England)	2
	Ernie Price	(England)	2
16	Alec Statham	(England)	0
	Ron Clarke	(England) (res)	2
	Lloyd Goffe	(England) (res)	(did not ride)
*	Wilf Jay	(England) (res)	(did not ride)

NB: *indicates that these riders had qualified from the Northern League.

1947 British Riders' Final

1	Jack Parker	(England)	14
2	Bill Kitchen	(England)	14
3	Bill Longley	(Australia)	11
4	Eric Chitty	(Canada)	10
5	George Wilks	(England)	9
6	Ernie Price	(England)	8
	Lionel Van Praag	(Australia)	8
	Vic Duggan	(Australia)	8
	Eric Langton	(England)	8
	Norman Parker	(England)	8
11	Tommy Price	(England)	6
	Ron Johnson	(Australia)	6
13	Les Wotton	(England)	4
	Geoff Pymar	(England)	4
15	Bill Pitcher	(England)	2
16	Frank Dolan	(Australia)	0
	Dent Oliver	(England) (res)	0
	Aub Lawson	(Australia) (res)	0

1948 British Riders' Final

1	Vic Duggan	(Australia)	14
2	Ron Johnson	(Australia)	13
3	Alec Statham	(England)	13
4	Bill Gilbert	(England)	10
	Split Waterman	(England)	10
6	Jack Parker	(England)	9
	Oliver Hart	(England)	9
8	Bill Longley	(Australia)	8
9	Wilbur Lamoreaux	(USA)	6
	Malcolm Craven	(England)	6
11	Jeff Lloyd	(England)	5
	Eric Chitty	(Canada)	5
	Lloyd Goffe	(England)	5
14	Ernie Price	(England)	4
15	Norman Parker	(England)	2
16	Dent Oliver	(England)	1
	Frank Hodgson	(England) (res)	0
	Jack Biggs	(Australia) (res)	(did not ride)

The World Championship 1949-69

Speedway's fortunes flowered, waned, and then revived during these two decades, but throughout the period world final night retained its charisma and glamour. The first English and Scandinavian world champions appeared, as the sport produced a host of unforgettable riders, including Jack Young, Peter Craven, Ronnie Moore, Ove Fundin, Barry Briggs, and Ivan Mauger.

The parade of riders at the first post war world final to be held. From left, Lloyd Goffe, Wilbur Lamoreaux, Bill Gilbert, Dent Oliver, Aub Lawson, Graham Warren, and Tommy Price.

33

1949
Tommy Price— England's first champion

AFTER AN ABSENCE of 10 years, the 1949 season saw the return of a genuine World Speedway Championship. In the years since the end of the war many more riders had become available, and were of the required standard. No less than 224 riders entered the preliminary rounds of the Championship, these contestants representing Britain, Australia, New Zealand, Norway, Sweden, Holland, Austria, America, Canada, and South Africa.

The first rounds on Third Division tracks catered for 160 riders, 96 of these going on to the Second Division rounds. Forty-eight riders qualified for the third round, and joined 32 of the lesser lights from the First Division for a further series of eliminators on Second Division circuits. From this exhausting programme the 10 leading scorers moved on to a final championship round where they were joined by 32 of the star riders from the First Division. At last, the 16 top scorers from these sessions moved forward to the big occasion at Wembley on 22 September.

The *Sunday Dispatch* again sponsored the final,

Tommy Price receives the champion's trophy from Mrs. Atlee, wife of the then Prime Minister. The popular Wembley rider was England's first winner of a world final.

Oliver Hart, one of the last leg-trailers, qualified as reserve, and provided great entertainment in the three rides that he took.

Score Chart

								Total
1	Tommy Price	England	3	3	3	3	3	15
2	Jack Parker	England	3	3	3	2	3	14
3	Louis Lawson	England	2	2	3	3	3	13
4	Norman Parker	England	3	3	2	2	0	10
5	Wilbur Lamoreaux	USA	2	2	3	ef	2	9
	Bill Kitchen	England	3	1	2	2	1	9
7	Ron Clarke	England	1	0	2	3	2	8
	Bill Longley	Australia	1	2	2	1	2	8
	Aub Lawson	Australia	1	3	1	1	2	8
10	Cyril Roger	England	2	0	1	1	3	7
11	Bill Gilbert	England	2	1	3	0	0	6
12	Graham Warren	Australia	0	2	exc	2	1	5
13	Ken Le Breton	Australia	1	0	1	1	1	4
14	Lloyd Goffe	England	0	1	ef	0	1	2
15	Cliff Watson	Australia	f	1	0	0	0	1
16	Dent Oliver	England	exc	0	ns	ns	ns	0
	Oliver Hart (res)	England				1	0	0	1
	Alec Statham (res)	England	(did not ride)					

Heat-by-heat

		Time
1	N Parker, Gilbert, Clarke, Watson (f)	75.4s
2	J Parker, Lamoreaux, Longley, Oliver (exc)	73.8s
3	Kitchen, Roger, Lawson, Warren	76.8s
4	Price, Lawson, LeBreton, Goffe	75.6s
5	Price, Warren, Watson, Oliver	75.8s
6	Lawson, Longley, Gilbert, LeBreton	77.2s
7	N Parker, Lamoreaux, Goffe, Roger	77.4s
8	J Parker, Lawson, Kitchen, Clarke	75.0s
9	Lawson, Longley, Roger, Watson	77.2s
10	Gilbert, Kitchen, Hart, Goffe (ef)	77.6s
11	Lamoreaux, Kitchen, LeBreton, Watson	78.4s
12	Price, Clarke, Lawson, Lamoreaux (ef)	78.2s
13	J Parker, N Parker, LeBreton, Warren (exc)	77.2s
14	Price, J Parker, Lawson, Hart	76.8s
16	Clarke, Warren, Longley, Goffe	78.4s
17	J Parker, Lawson, Goffe, Watson	77.2s
18	Lawson, Lamoreaux, Warren, Gilbert	77.4s
19	Price, Longley, Kitchen, N Parker	76.8s
20	Roger, Clarke, LeBreton, Hart	78.4s

providing a magnificent trophy and cash prizes for the top six riders, £500 going to the winner. A capacity crowd of 93,000 — many would-be spectators were unable to obtain tickets — crammed the stadium in anticipation of a great final. Some important names who had missed the championship rounds through injury were not present, however, including Vic Duggan, Ron Johnson, Freddie Williams, and Fred Tuck.

From the first race it was obvious that the old brigade of Tommy Price, Jack Parker, Norman Parker and Wilbur Lamoreaux was going to fill the major places by the end of the night. Price scored wins in heats four and five, his only real challenge in these races coming from young Louis Lawson, who proved to be the surprise packet of the evening. Price took advantage of a generous slice of luck in heat 12, winning the race after Lamoreaux's engine gave trouble while the latter was leading. Then the expected battle between Price and Jack Parker in heat 14 failed to materialise; Parker was slow away from the gate and was never really in contention, a circumstance that could be blamed on the effects of his having to run in heats 13 and 14 back-to-back. Thus Price emerged a worthy winner — a near veteran at 38 years of age, he was the first Englishman to be crowned world champion. In addition, he had had to fight his way through the preliminary rounds while suffering from a long bout of hay fever, but had still managed to head the list of qualifiers.

The Australian challengers were never in the hunt, their main hope, Graham Warren, appearing hopelessly at sea on the tight Wembley oval. His hopes of winning the title virtually disappeared in his first ride when he failed to make the gate, a mistake that usually proves disastrous among the elite company at Wembley. Of the other Aussies, Cliff Watson fell in his first outing and was never a serious threat after that, Bill Longley and Aub Lawson turned in moderate performances by their usual standards, and although Ken Le Breton was the first Second Division rider to appear in a world final, he tried hard but lacked the experience to make any impression on the big names.

Dent Oliver, one of England's great hopes, was not fully recovered from an injury he had sustained at West Ham just two nights previously. A fall and a last place in his first two rides convinced him that it was not to be his night. However Louis Lawson took his chances and was beaten only by Price and Jack Parker. His spectacular riding endeared him to the crowd and his third place gave England a 1-2-3 result, equalling the Americans' feat in 1937.

Norman Parker finished fourth in his best ever final, and but for Lamoreaux splitting him and Bill Kitchen England would have captured the top five placings. Lamoreaux was not on his best form, and minor mechanical problems added to his difficulties, robbing him of a better overall finishing place. Englishmen Bill Gilbert, Cyril Roger and Ron Clarke all performed much as expected and filled midfield positions, while the spectacular Oliver Hart took three of Dent Oliver's rides, and his inimitable leg-trailing style was a sheer joy to watch even if he did manage only one point.

1950
Williams—debut winner from Wales

ANOTHER ARDUOUS session of qualifying rounds faced competitors for the 1950 final. Rounds on Third Division tracks saw 128 riders from Second and Third Division teams, among them a few Continentals, fighting it out for the top 74 places. These riders then joined 52 Division Two contestants, and the leading 73 scorers from this group went forward to the third session of qualifying meetings. They met 38 First Division men and raced seven meetings on Second Division tracks, with the two highest scores from each of these events proceeding to the Championship rounds. Thirty-four of the big names from the First Division tracks, with the two highest scorers from each three rounds, and the top 16 scorers filtered through to Wembley.

The first major surprise of this season emerged from the Championship rounds, Second Division rider Jack Young besting all the First Division stars to break through as top qualifier with 39 points. Graham Warren and Cyril Brine followed the Edinburgh rider with 37 and 36 points respectively. Another Second

The 'blond bombshell', Graham Warren, in league action for Birmingham. Inset: from left, Wally Green, Fred Williams and Graham Warren.

Division rider, Arthur Forrest of Halifax, qualified as reserve, but injury prevented him from taking his place at Wembley. Notable names who failed to succeed in the qualifying rounds were Louis Lawson, Norman Parker, Alec Statham, George Wilks, and Malcolm Craven.

The final was wide open. Tommy Price and Jack Parker started as favourites, but there were unknown quantities in the shape of Young, 'Split' Waterman, Ronnie Moore and Freddie Williams, talented riders who were making their world final debuts. The illustrious Vic Duggan and the experienced Aub Lawson could not be discounted, and blond Warren had been displaying fine form for Birmingham.

As it transpired, the first heat at Wembley provided a pointer to the final reckoning. Welshman Williams won from the gate in what was to be the fastest time of the night, with West Ham's Wally Green in hot pursuit. The next heat saw the first major upset of the night, with Vic Duggan being relegated to third place. Price recorded a fast time in winning heat three, but with

Young in last place it was clear that 'Youngie' would not be on the rostrum when the racing was over. Warren won a terrific duel with Jack Parker in heat four, but heat five was to determine the fate of both Parker and Price. Badly away from the gate, Price tried to cut inside Dent Oliver and fell. Parker finished third, and having at that stage lost three points in two races he must have felt his chance of the title had slipped away.

Heats six, seven and eight saw the three young pretenders to the crown, Williams, Green and Warren, in winning form. Meanwhile Duggan scored two more lowly third places, and although Young began to find improved form it was too late for him to pose a serious threat. His win in his last race indicated that nerves had played a part in his earlier disappointing rides.

Warrren blew his chance of the title in heat 10, when he fell while trying to ride around Williams. As he had already won his first two outings, and went on to win his final two races, he could have been champion but for that incident. Williams beat the old track record for the second time during his tussle with Warren, yet in his next ride he allowed himself to be beaten by Parker, who recorded his only win of the night.

Warren's last two victories occurred in heats 16 and 17, one of his wins being over Green. Thus Warren's total was 12 points with all his rides completed, but Williams was on 11 and Green on 10, both having one more ride to come. Williams made no mistake in heat 18 by holding off a determined Moore and Price, thus inheriting the world championship. Green had the fiery Waterman and Lawson to contend with in heat 20, but he made no mistake and finished runner-up overall.

This had been Green's only appearance in a world final, and his performance was therefore all the more creditable. A young Danny Dunton was also making what was to be his sole appearance, but he managed only five points on a track he normally rode well. Moore provided signs of things to come in his future career by settling down to score seven points after two pointless initial outings. Even though he won heat 13, Price had obviously been affected by his earlier fall, but Waterman, with his distinctive wide handlebars and famous 'death dives' into the turns, proved equal to the task in his world final debut, scoring eight points. Old campaigner Lawson scored consistently in every race to finish fourth in the final point standings, but one rider who usually went well at Wembley, the lantern-jawed Australian Arthur Payne, just couldn't get it together and was obviously affected by big night nerves.

The 93,000 capacity crowd, equal to the 1949 attendance, saw the presentations made by Earl Mountbatten of Burma. An interesting comparison can be made between the ages of the top three riders in this final, and the ages of today's successful riders. Williams at 24, Green at 29, and the 25-year-old Warren were considered up-and-coming youngsters by the standards of the fifties, yet today they could be looked on as almost ancient.

Score Chart

								Total
1 Fred Williams	Wales	3	3	3	2	3		14
2 Wally Green	England	2	3	3	2	3		13
3 Graham Warren	Australia	3	3	f	3	3		12
4 Aub Lawson	Australia	2	2	3	1	2		10
5 Tommy Price	England	3	f	3	1	1		8
Jack Parker	England	2	1	2	3	0		8
Split Waterman	England	1	2	3	1	1		8
8 Jack Young	Australia	0	1	2	1	3		7
Cyril Brine	England	2	2	2	0	1		7
Ronnie Moore	New Zealand	exc	0	2	3	2		7
11 Dent Oliver	England	exc	3	1	2	0		6
12 Danny Dunton	England	1	0	1	1	2		5
13 Vic Duggan	Australia	1	1	1	0	1		4
14 Ron Clarke	England	1	2	0	0	0		3
Jack Biggs	Australia	0	1	0	0	2		3
16 Arthur Payne	Australia	0	0	exc	0	0		0
Cyril Roger (res)	England	3	2					5
Mike Erskine (res)	England	0						0

Heat-by-heat

		Time
1	Williams, Green, Clarke, Biggs	71.0s
2	Roger, Brine, Duggan, Payne (Oliver exc)	71.8s
3	Price, Lawson, Dunton, Young	71.4s
4	Warren, Parker, Waterman, Erskine (Moore exc)	71.6s
5	Oliver, Clarke, Parker, Price (f)	72.6s
6	Williams, Waterman, Duggan, Dunton	72.6s
7	Warren, Lawson, Biggs, Payne	72.2s
8	Green, Brine, Young, Moore	71.2s
9	Lawson, Moore, Duggan, Clarke	72.8s
10	Williams, Young, Oliver, Warren (f)	71.2s
11	Waterman, Roger, Young, Clarke (Payne exc)	72.6s
12	Green, Parker, Dunton, Payne	72.0s
13	Price, Brine, Waterman, Biggs	73.6s
14	Parker, Williams, Lawson, Brine	73.0s
15	Moore, Oliver, Dunton, Biggs	73.2s
16	Warren, Green, Price, Duggan	72.4s
17	Warren, Dunton, Brine, Clarke	72.2s
18	Williams, Moore, Price, Payne	73.8s
19	Young, Biggs, Duggan, Parker	73.8s
20	Green, Lawson, Waterman, Oliver	73.2s

1951
Jack Biggs lets the title drift away

THE 1951 FINAL will always be referred to as the one that Australian Jack Biggs did not win. However, proceedings started normally with the qualifying rounds on Division Two and Three tracks feeding the highest scoring riders into the Championship rounds. From these races Biggs captured the highest score of 29 points out of a possible 30, with Split Waterman on 27 and Alan Hunt collecting 26 points. Surprise non-qualifiers were Graham Warren, the bombshell of the previous year, Bill Kitchen, and Tommy Price, who was suffering from another bout of hay fever.

Another 93,000 crowd was preparing to fete Biggs as the new world champion when a dramatic turn of events brought them to their feet, and within a few minutes a completely new situation had developed.

When the riders lined up for heat 19 Biggs was the only man unbeaten at that late stage, and he needed only a third place to clinch the title. However, Aub Lawson took the lead while Biggs failed to make his usual rapid start and on the top bend found himself forced wide and into the rear of the three other riders.

New champion Jack Young corners feet-up.

He was blinded by the shale thrown up by his opponents, and was never able to pull up from last place.

Lawson maintained his lead to the final bend, when the irrepressible Waterman made a last-second challenge and rode round the Australian to beat him on the run-in to the flag. This gave Waterman 12 points, the same score as Biggs and Jack Young, and so a run-off was required to decide the desntation of the championship after it had seemed it was going to be Biggs's easy property.

Amid tremendous excitement the run-off got under way with Waterman lining up on the inside position, Biggs in the middle and Young in the outside slot. Biggs jetted into the lead and held it for a lap until he drifted wide, allowing Young to dive into the vacant space and hold his lead to the finish. In the meantime Waterman passed Biggs on the final turn to steal the runner-up spot from the disconsolate Australian.

Young had dropped his points to Biggs, Eddie Rigg and Ronnie Moore, while Waterman had been beaten

Jack Biggs, the man who got so close to a world title.

into third place by Rigg and Young in the first heat, and was again defeated in heat 15, this time by Jack Parker. Reigning champion Freddie Williams faded after his first ride.

Newcomers to the world final this year had been Rigg, Jeff Lloyd, Bob Leverenz, Hunt, Eric Williams, Ernie Roccio and first reserve Dick Bradley. Second reserve Geoff Mardon created an all-time record by being the only Division Three rider to reach a world final.

A notable feature of the meeting had been the really fast starting of Biggs. In his first four races he was troubled only once, in heat five when Young gave him a real tussle and finished only a bike's length behind. If Biggs could have repeated his rapid starts in the crucial heat 19 he might have won the title, but once he had gated slowly it was impossible to recover lost ground against riders of the calibre of Waterman, Lawson and Fred Williams.

Most of the races lacked the excitement which had been associated with previous Wembley finals, although Bradley certainly livened things up in heat 18 when he replaced the young American Roccio, who had aggravated an old injury. Only Louis Lawson was able to hold Bradley back in this race.

Norman Parker was a mere shadow of the rider who had contested the 1949 final, but veteran Jack Parker finished the night with three heat wins, and indeed his fine victory over Waterman in heat 15 proved to be costly for the latter — if he had won he would have taken the championship without the necessity for a run-off.

While the crowd sympathised with the demoralised Biggs, perhaps the most significant fact of the evening was that the neat and stylish Young became the only Second Division rider ever to win the World Speedway Championship. It's hard to imagine that this feat will ever be equalled.

Score Chart

								Total
1	Jack Young	Australia	2	2	3	3	2	12
2	Split Waterman	England	1	3	3	2	3	12
3	Jack Biggs	Australia	3	3	3	3	0	12
4	Ronnie Moore	New Zealand	2	2	2	2	3	11
5	Jack Parker	England	0	1	3	3	3	10
	Louis Lawson	England	2	0	2	3	3	10
7	Eddie Rigg	England	3	3	1	1	0	8
8	Aub Lawson	Australia	1	2	2	0	2	7
	Bob Leverenz	Australia	3	2	1	0	1	7
	Fred Williams	Wales	3	1	0	2	1	7
11	Eric Williams	Wales	0	1	1	2	2	6
	Jeff Lloyd	England	1	3	1	0	1	6
13	Norman Parker	England	0	1	1	1	0	3
	Cyril Brine	England	1	ef	2	0	0	3
15	Ernie Roccio	USA	2	0	0	ret	dns	2
	Alan Hunt	England	f	f	0	1	1	2
	Dick Bradley (res)	England					2	2
	Geoff Mardon (res)	New Zealand	(did not ride)					

Heat-by-heat

		Time
1	Rigg, Young, Waterman, N Parker	70.6s
2	Leverenz, Roccio, A Lawson, J Parker	71.0s
3	F Williams, L Lawson, Brine, E Williams	70.8s
4	Biggs, Moore, Lloyd, Hunt (f)	71.6s
5	Biggs, Young, J Parker, L Lawson	70.6s
6	Lloyd, A Lawson, N Parker, Brine (ef)	72.0s
7	Waterman, Moore, E Williams, Roccio	71.4s
8	Rigg, Leverenz, F Williams, Hunt (f)	71.6s
9	Young, A Lawson, E Williams, Hunt	70.6s
10	J Parker, Moore, N Parker, F Williams	71.2s
11	Young, F Williams, Lloyd, Roccio	71.4s
12	Biggs, Brine, Rigg, Roccio (ret)	71.2s
13	Waterman, L Lawson, Leverenz, Lloyd	72.2s
14	Biggs, E Williams, N Parker, Leverenz	72.2s
15	J Parker, Waterman, Hunt, Brine	72.4s
16	L Lawson, Moore, Rigg, A Lawson	71.8s
17	Moore, Young, Leverenz, Brine	72.0s
18	L Lawson, Bradley, Hunt, N Parker (Roccio dns)	73.2s
19	Waterman, A Lawson, F Williams, Biggs	73.2s
20	J Parker, E Williams, Lloyd, Rigg	73.8s
21	Young, Waterman, Biggs (run-off for first 3 places)	72.6s

1952
A Young man's record—setting night

Bob Oakley finished third in the only world final he contested.

AN INNOVATION in qualifying procedures marked the 1952 season, when Continental riders were granted their own eliminating rounds in deference to their improving strength. Early meetings were held in West Germany and Norway, with further Scandinavian qualifiers being staged in Denmark, Norway, Sweden and Finland. These sessions led up to the Scandinavian Final in Oslo and the Continental Final in Munich, from which meetings the best riders won through to the European Grand Final at Falkoping in Sweden. Also contrary to tradition, five British riders were despatched to ride in these Continental and Scandinavian meetings. But of Reg Morgan, Bob Mark, Jim Gregory, Ken McKinlay and Tony Lewis, only Gregory progressed on to the British International qualifiers.

At home, the top 24 from 96 competitors in the first National rounds got through to the International section, where they were joined by six men from Falkoping and 66 riders from Division One and Two tracks. The top 60 then entered the Championship rounds on Division One tracks, where 20 top riders from the First Division added to the action. Each rider had two qualifying meetings, the top scorers being Bob Oakley on 28, and Jack Young, Split Waterman, Ronnie Moore, and Freddie Williams all on 27.

The line-up for the Wembley final was truly international for the first time since the war. Henry Long from South Africa and Dan Forsberg from Sweden were representing their countries for the first time in world finals, while Basse Hveem was the first Norwegian to travel to Wembley even though, as reserve, he was not called upon to ride.

The fans were wondering whether Jack Young could repeat his victory of 1951. He had now entered First Division racing by joining West Ham, and this experience enabled him to cope better with big night pressures. As Split Waterman was handicapped by a cracked knee cap and top qualifier Bob Oakley was an unknown quantity at world championship level, it was anyone's guess as to which rider would walk away with the trophy. Newcomers to the world final were Derek Close, Ron How, Arthur Forrest, Brian Crutcher, Forsberg, Long, and the two reserves Hveem and Trevor Redmond. Missing from the occasion were stalwarts of the past such as the Parker brothers, Bill Kitchen, Tommy Price, and Aub Lawson.

The meeting was not as exciting as some of the earlier finals had been, although technically it represented speedway at its best. The way in which Young appeared almost casual in his defence of his title showed the hallmark of a true champion. He was truly in a class of his own that night.

As a meeting of great riders, however, the event certainly lived up to its reputation with a genuinely cosmopolitan representation of countries. Fred Williams and Oakley, both riding on their home league track, finished second and third, partly because they so obviously conquered the terrors of the starting gate. Forrest, the 'Black Prince', also proved he had a lot to offer with fine performances in his last two rides. Neither did Forsberg disgrace himself or Sweden; his

Score Chart

							Total
1 Jack Young	Australia	3	3	3	3	2	14
2 Fred Williams	Wales	3	2	3	2	3	13
3 Bob Oakley	England	3	3	2	1	3	12
4 Ronnie Moore	New Zealand	2	2	3	f	3	10
5 Arthur Payne	Australia	0	1	2	3	3	9
Dan Forsberg	Sweden	2	3	1	3	f/r	9
Dick Bradley	England	3	2	3	1	0	9
8 Jeff Lloyd	England	2	2	0	2	1	7
Arthur Forrest	England	1	1	0	3	2	7
Henry Long	South Africa	1	0	2	2	2	7
11 Brian Crutcher	England	1	3	1	0	1	6
Split Waterman	England	2	1	0	1	2	6
13 Graham Warren	Australia	0	1	1	2	1	5
14 Derek Close	England	1	0	2	0	1	4
15 Cyril Roger	England	0	exc	1	1	0	2
16 Ron How	England	0	ef	0	0	0	0
Basse Hveem (res)	Norway	(did not ride)					
Trevor Redmond (res)	New Zealand	(did not ride)					

Heat-by-heat

		Time
1	Williams, Moore, Close, Payne⁷	69.6s
2	Oakley, Lloyd, Forrest, How	70.4s
3	Young, Forsberg, Long, Warren	70.4s
4	Bradley, Waterman, Crutcher, Roger	71.2s
5	Crutcher, Lloyd, Warren, Close	71.8s
6	Young, Williams, Waterman, How (ef)	70.6s
7	Forsberg, Moore, Forrest, Roger (exc)	70.2s
8	Oakley, Bradley, Payne, Long	70.6s
9	Bradley, Close, Forsberg, How	71.4s
10	Williams, Long, Roger, Lloyd	71.0s
11	Moore, Oakley, Warren, Waterman	70.6s
12	Young, Payne, Crutcher, Forrest	71.4s
13	Forrest, Long, Waterman, Close	71.2s
14	Forsberg, Williams, Oakley, Crutcher	71.6s
15	Young, Lloyd, Bradley, Moore (f)	72.4s
16	Payne, Warren, Roger, How	72.2s
17	Oakley, Young, Close, Roger	72.0s
18	Williams, Forrest, Warren, Bradley	72.4s
19	Moore, Long, Crutcher, How	72.4s
20	Payne, Waterman, Lloyd, Forsberg (f/re)	72.2s

Two great riders of the 1950s, Ronnie Moore (leading) and Jack Young in close quarters. Young's 1952 victory made him the first double winner in world final history.

outstanding ride of the night was his victory in heat 14 over Williams and Oakley. At that time both the latter were in contention for the championship, and Forsberg's fall in the final heat robbed him of a possible run-off with Oakley for third place overall.

If there had been an award for courage it would have gone to Waterman, who defied doctor's orders to race, and although in great pain from his injury he rode hard for his six points. Another outstanding performance came from the youngest rider in the final, 18-year-old Brian Crutcher. His tenacity overcame his obvious nerves when he provided the finest race of the night in heat five as he waited until the last bend to snatch victory from Jeff Lloyd.

The following race saw a masterful display of tactics by Young that thrilled another capacity crowd. Young missed the gate and followed Waterman and Williams on the first lap. Passing Waterman, Young then got to grips with the flying Welshman. Young pulled out every trick in the book, trying inside and outside lines, but always being countered by the wily Williams. The battle of wits and speed rocked the huge crowd, and an even bigger roar than usual echoed around the stadium as Young appeared almost to throw his machine past his rival going down the back straight on the final lap. They took the last bend neck and neck, but Young gained the verdict at the flag by the width of a tyre.

For the record book Young's classic performance made him the first rider to win the World Championship twice. He had also achieved the feat in successive years. The first part of that record was soon to be shared, but it was to be six years before the second part was equalled, and 18 seasons before it was bettered.

1953
Williams rocks the title favourites

THE BIG QUESTION everyone was asking prior to the 1953 World Final was: could Jack Young make it a hat-trick of victories? The query was justified, too, for Ronnie Moore was in great form for Wimbledon, Split Waterman was riding better than he had ever done, and teenager Brian Crutcher was improving weekly.

By now the system of qualifying rounds had settled down into an established pattern, with the Continental meetings producing their share of finalists, and the British rounds sorting out the best home-based riders. New Zealander Moore led the home qualifiers, while the Swedes were represented by Olle Nygren and Rune Sormander. Moore was probably the favourite, but Young was obviously determined to remain in the driving seat, and the stage was set for a great final.

A 90,000 crowd arrived to watch the outcome, and if they were seeking shocks they had to wait no longer than the first heat. Freddie Williams came from the back to beat Dick Bradley, while Crutcher languished

Split Waterman, the English hope who twice finished runner-up in world finals, rides inside Louis Lawson.

in third place and Sormander was last. Young won the second heat with comparative ease from Arthur Forrest, while Waterman showed he meant business by taking heat three.

Heat four delivered the next shock, when Moore fell on the first lap, leaving Geoff Mardon to win. The next race was crucial, bringing together Williams, Young and Moore. It turned into a tremendous spectacle as Williams proved that he knew how to beat the impeccable Young on the tricky Wembley track, and Moore almost passed the reigning champion on the final run-in to the flag. Waterman, again in a determined mood, won heat six comfortably from Mardon, who was turning into the surprise package.

Williams won heat nine from Graham Warren, who had his best race of the night, while Waterman took heat 12 from Moore, who seemed to have recovered some of his confidence after that first race fall. Another big surprise arrived in heat 13, when Jeff Lloyd gained a flyer from the start and Williams was unable to catch the Harringay man. To be fair, it should be remembered that the race was started by the green light as the gate had failed, and Williams seemed unhappy at what turned into a ragged start.

Heat 15 was another vital race, as it brought together Waterman and Young. The starting gate was still out of action, and from the green light Waterman streaked into the first turn like a rocket, with Young left badly behind. Young set out in pursuit of Bradley, but took three laps to catch him. On the last lap he also stormed past Eric Chitty, but there was no way that he could overhaul the flying Waterman. Young was clearly not at his best on the greasy track, and must also have been cursing the inoperative starting gate, for by now he had dropped two points and his chance of a third world championship had almost certainly gone.

At this stage the pattern of the evening's racing had formed: heat 17 was to be all-important, as it would bring together the so far unbeaten Waterman, Williams, who had dropped only one point, and Nygren, the hard riding Swede who was shaping up as a potential spoiler. Happily the starting gate was brought back into operation for this race, but as the riders cruised up to the tapes Waterman suddenly pulled up with clutch trouble. The warning for the two-minute allowance was sounded, and with just seconds to spare Waterman rolled up to the gate.

From the gate Williams and Nygren burst into the lead, crowding Waterman out on the first turn. Waterman made supreme efforts to pass Nygren, but the tough Swede thwarted every move, and Williams won the race with the unlucky Waterman left in third place. Freddie Williams thus became the second rider to win the world title twice.

Meanwhile New Zealander Mardon had been totting up the points, and he equalled Nygren's score for the evening by winning heat 20, in which Young fell and ruined his last chance of a place on the rostrum. In the run-off for third place, Mardon won as Nygren fell.

Score Chart

								Total
1 Fred Williams	Wales		3	3	3	2	3	14
2 Split Waterman	England		3	3	3	3	1	13
3 Geoff Mardon	New Zealand		3	2	3	1	3	12
Olle Nygren	Sweden		2	3	2	3	2	12
5 Jack Young	Australia		3	2	3	2	f	10
6 Ronnie Moore	New Zealand		f	1	2	3	3	9
7 Jeff Lloyd	England		2	2	f/e	3	1	8
8 Arthur Forrest	England		2	2	0	0	3	7
Aub Lawson	Australia		1	3	2	1	0	7
10 Brian Crutcher	England		1	1	1	2	1	6
11 Rune Sormander	Sweden		0	0	1	2	2	5
Graham Warren	Australia		0	0	2	1	2	5
13 Eric Williams	Wales		1	1	1	1	f	4
14 Alan Hunt	England		0	0	1	0	2	3
15 Dick Bradley	England		2	f/r	0	0	0	2
16 Jack Biggs	Australia		1	1	f/e	0	ns	2
Dent Oliver (res)	England						1	1
Arthur Payne (res)	Australia		(did not ride)					
Louis Lawson (res)	England		(did not ride)					
Maury Dunn (res)	New Zealand		(did not ride)					

Heat-by-heat

		Time
1	F Williams, Bradley, Crutcher, Sormander	70.4s
2	Young, Forrest, Lawson, Warren	71.0s
3	Waterman, Lloyd, Biggs, Hunt	73.2s
4	Mardon, Nygren, E Williams, Moore (f)	72.2s
5	F Williams, Young, Moore, Hunt	70.8s
6	Waterman, Mardon, Crutcher, Warren	72.8s
7	Nygren, Forrest, Biggs, Bradley (f/re)	73.8s
8	Lawson, Lloyd, E Williams, Sormander	72.6s
9	F Williams, Warren, E Williams, Biggs (f/exc)	72.8s
10	Young, Nygren, Crutcher, Lloyd (f/exc)	73.2s
11	Mardon, Lawson, Hunt, Bradley	74.2s
12	Waterman, Moore, Sormander, Forrest	72.0s
13	Lloyd, F Williams, Mardon, Forrest	73.2s
14	Moore, Crutcher, Lawson, Biggs	72.6s
15	Waterman, Young, E Williams, Bradley	72.6s
16	Nygren, Sormander, Warren, Hunt	74.6s
17	F Williams, Nygren, Waterman, Lawson	73.0s
18	Forrest, Hunt, Crutcher (f/re), E Williams (f)	74.6s
19	Moore, Warren, Lloyd, Bradley	74.2s
20	Mardon, Sormander, Oliver, Young (f), Biggs (ns)	75.0s
21	Mardon beat Nygren in run-off for 3rd place	74.2s

Freddie Williams, champion for the second time.

43

1954 Wembley's greatest night?

THIS WAS to be the last year that British rounds dominated the qualifying procedure for the World Final. Although the Continentals had been holding their own qualifiers for two seasons now, their successful riders had never been seeded direct to Wembley, but had had to battle it out through the British Championship rounds. Only if they managed to get among the top 16 scorers at these events could they race at Wembley.

In 1954 Olle Nygren and the unknown 21-year-old, Ove Fundin, were the Continentals — in fact, both were Swedes — who got through to the final. The major surprise from the qualifying rounds was the failure of reigning champion Freddie Williams to reach the highest scoring 16. He was included as second reserve, but even that was only after he had won a run-off against Gerald Hussey.

Although this was considered to be one of the most open finals to date only 80,000 tickets were sold for the occasion. Jack Young was probably the most favoured rider to win, but Brian Crutcher, Nygren, Split Waterman, Eddie Rigg, Arthur Forrest and Ronnie Moore were all in fine form. Moore had to ride with a special appliance fitted to a leg he had fractured some 10 weeks previously.

Only two races had been run before it became obvious that the challenge from the much fancied Bradford duo of Forrest and Rigg was not to materialise. Forrest tailed in last in heat one, and Rigg did likewise in heat two. To make matters worse for the northern contingent, Belle Vue's Peter Craven fell in heat three. The way in which England's Fred Brand

Arthur Forrest, the renowned 'Black Prince', proved a disappointment, failing to score in two of his heats and ending with only a five-point total.

44

had won the first race made it seem that a night of upsets was definitely on.

Crutcher and Young each won his first outing, while Moore also achieved a win in his first event, coming from the back in heat four after a bad gate. From their mediocre performances in these heats, it also seemed as though the chances of Tommy Price, Barry Briggs, Jack Biggs, Trevor Redmond and Fundin had also disappeared. A last place in heat five further sealed the fate of Craven.

Still in with a chance were the winners of the four opening heats, Brand, Crutcher, Young and Moore, while Aub Lawson, Geoff Mardon, Nygren and Waterman had dropped only one point each. Heat six proved to be not only the toughest race of the night, but also the turning point in this final. Four potential champions, Lawson, Crutcher, Young and Moore cruised up to the line and settled down at the tapes. Crouching over his bike, Moore made no mistake when the tapes went up, streaking into the lead. Although twinges of pain from his injured leg were sapping his concentration, he moved further ahead, unaware of the tremendous battle taking place behind him. Crutcher and Young, level on points at that stage, were fighting it out with the former slightly in front. Crutcher rode his young heart out, foxing every tactical move made by Young and holding on to second place until the flag. Lawson's last place put him out of the running, while Young's chances were now fading fast.

Nygren won heat seven from a very wild Briggs, but Waterman's third place knocked him out of contention. Heat nine brought Nygren and Crutcher together in an important clash, but Crutcher's relative inexperience cost him a point when he failed to take advantage of slips made by Nygren and Biggs early in the race. Nygren won from Crutcher, with Biggs third. Although Waterman won heat ten, it was obvious at this halfway stage that Moore, Crutcher and Nygren were the main challengers, with Young holding only an outside chance of winning the title.

Moore went on to win heats 11 and 13, Young took races 12 and 15, and Nygren maintained the pressure with success in heat 14. Then Young finally blew what remained of his opportunities by finishing behind Forrest and Waterman in heat 17.

World champion at his fifth attempt, Ronnie Moore with Brian Crutcher (centre) and Olle Nygren.

This left Nygren needing to beat Moore in the final heat to enforce a run-off for the title, but the expected classic race did not materialise. Moore sped from the gate and was 40 yards up on Nygren at the end of the first lap. He finished the race as the new World Champion while Nygren was still riding around the last bend. This meant that the Swede and Crutcher met in a run-off to decide the second and third overall placings, but this race proved to be as hollow a spectacle as heat 20, with Crutcher leding all the way.

Unknown to the crowds, they had just witnessed the start of a new era in speedway history with the 1954 debuts of Briggs, Fundin and Craven. In future years this trio were destined to win no less than 11 finals between them. Adding to these names those of the new champion Ronnie Moore and former title holders Tommy Price, Fred Williams, and Jack Young meant that the 1954 meeting had included probably the most illustrious field that had ever contested a World Speedway Final.

Score Chart

								Total
1	Ronnie Moore	New Zealand	3	3	3	3	3	15
2	Brian Crutcher	England	3	2	2	3	3	13
3	Olle Nygren	Sweden	2	3	3	3	2	13
4	Jack Young	Australia	3	1	3	3	1	11
5	Split Waterman	England	2	1	3	1	2	9
	Barry Briggs	New Zealand	1	2	2	2	2	9
7	Eddie Rigg	England	0	3	2	2	0	7
	Fred Brand	England	3	1	0	2	1	7
	Jack Biggs	Australia	1	3	1	1	1	7
10	Arthur Forrest	England	0	1	0	1	3	5
	Geoff Mardon	New Zealand	2	2	1	0	0	5
	Tommy Price	England	1	0	2	0	2	5
	Trevor Redmond	New Zealand	f	2	1	1	1	5
14	Aub Lawson	Australia	2	0	0	2	0	4
15	Peter Craven	England	f	0	0	0	3	3
16	Ove Fundin	Sweden	1	0	1	0	f/e	2
	Alan Hunt (res)	England	(did not ride)					
	Fred Williams (res)	Wales	(did not ride)					

Heat-by-heat

		Time
1	Brand, Lawson, Price, Forrest	71.8s
2	Crutcher, Mardon, Briggs, Rigg	71.0s
3	Young, Nygren, Fundin, Craven (f)	71.2s
4	Moore, Waterman, Biggs, Redmond (f)	71.2s
5	Rigg, Redmond, Forrest, Craven	72.6s
6	Moore, Crutcher, Young, Lawson	72.0s
7	Nygren, Briggs, Waterman, Price	72.0s
8	Biggs, Mardon, Brand, Fundin	72.2s
9	Nygren, Crutcher, Biggs, Forrest	72.0s
10	Waterman, Rigg, Fundin, Lawson	72.2s
11	Moore, Price, Mardon, Craven	71.6s
12	Young, Briggs, Redmond, Brand	72.0s
13	Moore, Briggs, Forrest, Fundin	72.4s
14	Nygren, Lawson, Redmond, Mardon	73.6s
15	Young, Rigg, Biggs, Price	71.6s
16	Crutcher, Brand, Waterman, Craven	72.4s
17	Forrest, Waterman, Young, Mardon	72.2s
18	Craven, Briggs, Biggs, Lawson	72.6s
19	Crutcher, Price, Redmond, Fundin (f/exc)	73.2s
20	Moore, Nygren, Brand, Rigg	72.6s
21	Crutcher beat Nygren in run-off for 2nd place	72.4s

1955
Peter Craven, king of balance

FOR THE FIRST TIME in the history of the championship, the Continental countries were this season permitted to seed riders direct to Wembley. Four Continentals were allocated places at Wembley, and these were taken by the top scorers in the European Grand Final at Oslo, the successful riders being Olle Nygren, Ove Fundin and Kjell Carlsson from Sweden, and Norwegian Henry Andersen.

The British qualifying rounds were run on similar lines to previous years, and the leading scorers were Peter Craven and Jack Young, each with 29 points out of a possible 30, and Barry Briggs on 28. A surprise package was New Zealander Ron Johnston — not to be confused with the Australian Ron Johnson who had featured in pre-war world finals and post-war British Riders Championships — on 26 points, a score equalled by reigning world champion Ronnie Moore.

The dynamic Peter Craven won the first of his two world titles in 1955.

With Nygren, and to a lesser degree the improving Fundin, this group constituted the favourites for the 1955 final.

The final again attracted less than a capacity crowd, the new commercial channel on television being blamed for keeping the public indoors. Nevertheless the atmosphere at Wembley was as intense as ever. Predictably, Moore won the first heat from Brian Crutcher and Arthur Wright, but a real shock emerged in heat two when the tiny Peter Craven balanced his way round the Empire Stadium to win, hardly putting his feet down as he recorded what was to the fastest time of the night. Nygren virtually put himself out of contention by finishing last in this race, but his fellow countryman Fundin kept his hopes alive by taking second place.

Briggs, still a little erratic in these early days of his career, won heat four from little opposition, but in the next race Crutcher dropped his second point of the night when he was beaten by Young. Then in heat six Nygren beat both Briggs and Moore, so at that stage the final was still wide open.

Another scintillating ride and a fast time by Craven in heat eight kept him in the reckoning, while Crutcher hit back to beat Nygren in heat nine, and Moore, assisted by Eric Williams, relegated Fundin to third place in heat ten. Thus, by the halfway mark only Craven remained unbeaten.

The next race radically altered the situation, however, when Briggs beat Craven, who even had a hard job in keeping Young back in third place. But certainly, Craven's thrilling riding was giving the crowd plenty of cheer about. Heat 13 saw Eric Williams beat Briggs after Crutcher had been excluded for his riding tactics in what most spectators thought was a hard decision. It meant that Crutcher's chances had now disappeared. A majestic struggle took place in heat 14 between Craven and Moore, with the former winning. Craven had now dropped only one point, while Briggs had missed two and Moore had lost three.

Fundin won heat 15 in fine style, and looked as though he might prove a spoiler when he met Briggs in the final race. And when Young took heat 16 to put himself only three points behind Craven, excitement was mounting as the last four heats loomed up.

Craven, the wizard of balance, tried every ploy possible to get past Crutcher in heat 17, but was unsuccessful. This meant that only Briggs could equal Craven's total of 13 points, and he had a tough contest coming up in heat 20. Moore beat Young in heat 18, and then Eric Williams, the surprise of the night, bested Nygren in the next race.

This left a dramatic situation in that if Briggs won heat 20, two run-offs would be required to settle the top three placings, one between himself and Craven for the championship itself, and another between Moore and Williams to decide third position.

The atmosphere was electric for heat 20 — the crowd was on Craven's side and hoped for any result other than a win by Briggs. And they had plenty to cheer about when Fundin made a good gate and held on despite four laps of desperate riding by Briggs. Thus Craven was champion, and a more popular one there had not been since Bluey Wilkinson won in 1938.

The nerve-tingling run-off for the other placings on the rostrum saw Moore jet from the gate and lead all the way. But behind him a tremendous battle raged between Briggs and Williams, resulting in a tangle on the final bend. Briggs wound it all on and collided with Williams; both riders went sprawling, but Briggs was fortunate to be able to restart his machine and ride past the flag. Williams, however, pushed home because he was convinced, as was a majority of the crowd, that Briggs would be excluded for his riding tactics. But the results were allowed to stand, and Briggs was declared third behind Craven and Moore.

Eric Williams's fourth place was all the more creditable in that he had originally travelled to Wembley only as a reserve.

Score Chart

									Total
1	Peter Craven	England	3	3	2	3	2	13
2	Ronnie Moore	New Zealand	3	1	3	2	3	12
3	Barry Briggs	New Zealand	3	2	3	2	2	12
	Eric Williams	Wales	3	1	2	3	3	12
5	Brian Crutcher	England	2	2	3	f/e	3	10
	Ove Fundin	Sweden	2	1	1	3	3	10
	Jack Young	Australia	1	3	1	3	2	10
8	Olle Nygren	Sweden	0	3	2	2	2	9
9	Arthur Forrest	England	0	2	3	1	1	7
10	Billy Bales	England	2	0	1	2	1	6
	Ron Johnston	New Zealand	1	1	2	1	1	6
	Arthur Wright	England	1	3	0	1	1	6
13	Kjell Carlsson	Sweden	0	2	0	1	0	3
14	Henry Andersen	Norway	1	0	1	0	0	2
	Phil Clarke	England	2	0	0	0	0	2
16	Cyril Roger	England	0	0	0	0	f/e	0
	Ken McKinlay (res)	Scotland	(did not ride)					
	Gerald Hussey (res)	England	(did not ride)					

NB: Aub Lawson and Doug Davies qualified but were unable to ride.

Heat-by-heat

		Time
1	Moore, Crutcher, Wright, Forrest	70.4s
2	Craven, Fundin, Johnston, Nygren	69.2s
3	Williams, Bales, Young, Carlsson	71.2s
4	Briggs, Clarke, Andersen, Roger	70.4s
5	Young, Crutcher, Fundin, Clarke	71.2s
6	Nygren, Briggs, Moore, Bales	70.8s
7	Wright, Carlsson, Johnston, Roger	72.0s
8	Craven, Forrest, Williams, Andersen	70.8s
9	Crutcher, Nygren, Andersen, Carlsson	71.4s
10	Moore, Williams, Fundin, Roger	71.4s
11	Briggs, Craven, Young, Wright	70.4s
12	Forrest, Johnston, Bales, Clarke	72.2s
13	Williams, Briggs, Johnston, Crutcher (f/exc)	72.0s
14	Craven, Moore, Carlsson, Clarke	70.8s
15	Fundin, Bales, Wright, Andersen	72.4s
16	Young, Nygren, Forrest, Roger	72.0s
17	Crutcher, Craven, Bales, Roger (f/exc)	71.6s
18	Moore, Young, Johnston, Andersen	72.0s
19	Williams, Nygren, Wright, Clarke	73.2s
20	Fundin, Briggs, Forrest, Carlsson	72.6s
21	Moore beat Briggs and Williams in run-off for 2nd and 3rd places	71.6s

1956
New champion, new country, new night

TWO IMPORTANT changes in the qualifying procedure were introduced for the 1956 season. It was decided to seed the reigning world champion — in this instance Peter Craven — direct to the final. Craven may have lost financially by not having to contest the preliminary rounds, but at least he could be certain that mechanical failures or other unforeseen problems would not prevent him from appearing at Wembley. The practice of seeding the best Continental riders direct from their own final was continued, and this year four Swedish riders — Continental champion Ove Fundin, Peo Soderman, Ulf Ericsson and Olle Andersson II — moved forward to Wembley from the Oslo event.

The other major modification involved a switch from a Thursday night to a Saturday for the Wembley final.

Runner-up Ronnie Moore leads Alan Hunt, who scored six points.

Sweden's four finalists in 1956, from left, Peo Soderman, Ove Fundin, Olle Andersson and Ulf Ericsson.

This assisted riders travelling from distant tracks and countries, and was also intended to boost spectator attendance. With a crowd of 65,000 this move appeared to have had some success, and with a good line-up of riders matters seemed set for an eventful night's racing.

In beating Ronnie Moore and Fundin in the first heat, Craven set a race time of 72.0 seconds, which was almost two seconds faster than any other heat time that was to be recorded that evening. The first upset came in heat two, when the highly rated Brian Crutcher was relegated to third place behind Arthur Forrest and Second Division rider Ken McKinlay. With Barry Briggs winning heat four, a battle of the giants seemed set.

Heat six brought together Craven, Briggs, Crutcher,

Score Chart

								Total
1	Ove Fundin	Sweden	1	3	3	3	3	13
2	Ronnie Moore	New Zealand	2	2	2	3	3	12
3	Arthur Forrest	England	3	1	3	2	2	11
	Peter Craven	England	3	1	2	2	3	11
5	Ken McKinlay	Scotland	2	2	3	3	f	10
	Barry Briggs	New Zealand	3	2	1	3	1	10
	Peo Soderman	Sweden	0	3	2	2	3	10
8	Brian Crutcher	England	1	3	3	f/e	2	9
9	Peter Moore	Australia	2	1	1	2	2	8
10	Eric Boothroyd	England	2	3	1	1	0	7
11	Alan Hunt	England	3	ef	1	1	1	6
12	Dick Fisher	England	0	f	2	1	2	5
13	Doug Davies	South Africa	1	2	0	0	1	4
14	Ulf Ericsson	Sweden	0	0	0	1	1	2
	Olle Andersson II	Sweden	1	1	0	0	0	2
16	Gerald Hussey	England	f	0	0	0	0	0
	Jack Biggs (res)	Australia	(did not ride)					
	Nigel Boocock (res)	England	(did not ride)					

NB: The reserve positions were decided in a run-off at Wembley a week before the final. Peter Moore beat Biggs and Boocock to take the one available place in the line-up. The other two riders were declared reserves.

Heat-by-heat

		Time
1	Craven, R Moore, Fundin, Soderman	72.0s
2	Forrest, McKinlay, Crutcher, Fisher	74.2s
3	Hunt, Boothroyd, Andersson, Ericsson	75.8s
4	Briggs, P Moore, Davies, Hussey (f)	75.4s
5	Soderman, Davies, Forrest, Ericsson	73.8s
6	Crutcher, Briggs, Craven, Hunt (ef)	75.2s
7	Boothroyd, R Moore, P Moore, Fisher (f)	74.8s
8	Fundin, McKinlay, Andersson, Hussey	75.6s
9	Crutcher, Soderman, Boothroyd, Hussey	74.6s
10	Forrest, Craven, P Moore, Andersson	74.8s
11	McKinlay, R Moore, Briggs, Ericsson	74.2s
12	Fundin, Fisher, Hunt, Davies	75.8s
13	Briggs, Soderman, Fisher, Andersson	74.6s
14	McKinlay, Craven, Boothroyd, Davies	74.8s
15	R Moore, Forrest, Hunt, Hussey	75.0s
16	Fundin, P Moore, Ericsson, Crutcher (f/exc)	76.2s
17	Soderman, P Moore, Hunt, McKinlay (f)	75.2s
18	Craven, Fisher, Ericsson, Hussey	75.2s
19	R Moore, Crutcher, Davies, Andersson	74.8s
20	Fundin, Forrest, Briggs, Boothroyd	75.6s
21	Forrest beat Craven in run-off for 3rd place	76.0s

and heat three winner Alan Hunt. Craven gated first and was leading easily until he suffered the cruel blow of a blown engine on the last lap. This allowed Crutcher to win from Briggs, while Craven was able to salvage a point because Hunt had already retired from the race. Eric Boothroyd delivered another shock in heat seven by beating Moore, and in heat eight Fundin won from a persistent McKinlay. Crutcher took heat nine, but when Craven used a borrowed machine in heat 10 he was unable to pass Forrest.

At this half-way stage it was still anyone's final, with none of the leading contenders remaining unbeaten. McKinlay further upset predictions with a fine win over Moore and Briggs in heat 11, and Fundin maintained his pressure with a victory in heat 12. Then Briggs pulled back into the reckoning with success in heat 13.

McKinlay beat Craven in heat 14, and for the second time in Wembley history it looked like a Second Division rider might win the title. The Scot had gained 10 points from his first four rides, and had his easiest outing still to come. Moore won heat 15 to put himself level on points with Forrest, whom he beat in that ride, and Fundin made no mistake in heat 16, after Crutcher had been excluded and put himself right out of the reckoning.

With each rider having just one race left, McKinlay and Fundin were on 10 points, Moore, Briggs and Forrest had nine, while Craven had scored only eight and thus had everything to go for. Of the leaders, McKinlay was first to make his last ride, in heat 17. He pulled out an easy lead, but fell when there was no pressure on him, and although he remounted he could do no better than last place. Craven, still on a borrowed bike, won heat 18 to finish with 11 points, and heat 19 saw Moore beat a disheartened Crutcher to finish with an 11-point total.

Everything now depended on the last race. If Briggs won from Fundin they would both join Moore on 12 points, while Forrest could also reach the 12-point mark if he could win. It was a tremendous finale to what had been a tense meeting.

In the event, Fundin made it an unexciting race by streaking into a lead that was never to be seriously challenged. Forrest rode well to keep Briggs at bay, leaving Boothroyd to bring up the rear. So Fundin became the new champion and Moore was second. In the run-off for third place, Forrest just got the better of Craven. One wonders what might have happened if Craven had not suffered engine trouble in his second ride — even Fundin would have conceded that the end result might have been different if the Englishman had not had to borrow machinery for most of the night.

Of the newcomers to world final racing, McKinlay proved that he could hold his own in top class company, and Peter Moore and Boothroyd both scored consistently. Dick Fisher lost form after a crash in heat seven, and Doug Davies, who had missed the 1955 event because of illness, was disappointing apart from a strong second place in heat five. Old campaigner Jack Biggs (remember 1951?) and newcomer Nigel Boocock were the reserves, but were not called upon to ride.

1957
Fundin slips, Barry Briggs steps in

FEW CHANGES to the qualifying system were made for this season, although the British eliminating rounds were raced off in the only league that was still operating at that time. Two semi-finals at Coventry and Belle Vue sent the top 11 scorers to Wembley, where they met the five best men from the Continental Final at Vaxjo in Sweden, which was won by Rune Sormander.

One notable difference this year was that for the first time since the World Speedway Championship had been instituted, Wembley stood as a 'neutral' track. The famous Wembley Lions had ceased to operate as a league team, and the fact that all riders would have to race on level terms pleased the minority faction in speedway that had always felt that the Wembley league riders had had an advantage on the big nights in the Empire Stadium.

With eight nations represented, an interesting final was expected, the favourites being reigning champion

Score Chart

								Total
1 Barry Briggs	New Zealand	3	2	3	3	3	14
2 Ove Fundin	Sweden	3	3	2	3	3	14
3 Peter Craven	England	2	1	3	2	3	11
4 Aub Lawson	Australia	3	3	1	2	2	11
Rune Sormander	Sweden	1	3	3	1	3	11
6 Ron Johnston	New Zealand	3	2	1	1	2	9
7 Ken McKinlay	Scotland	0	0	3	3	2	8
Bob Roger	England	2	1	2	2	1	8
9 Jack Geran	Australia	1	3	1	1	1	7
Ron How	England	1	2	2	f/e	2	7
Peo Soderman	Sweden	1	2	0	3	1	7
12 Aage Hansen	Norway	0	0	2	2	0	4
George White	England	2	1	0	1	0	4
14 Ian Williams	Wales	2	0	1	0	0	3
15 Dan Forsberg	Sweden	0	1	0	f	1	2
16 Josef Hofmeister	W Germany	f/r	f	0	0	0	0
Brian Crutcher (res)	England	(did not ride)					
Jack Biggs (res)	Australia	(did not ride)					

Heat-by-heat

		Time
1	Fundin, Craven, Sormander, McKinlay	71.2s
2	Lawson, Williams, Geran, Hofmeister (f/re)	72.2s
3	Briggs, White, Soderman, Forsberg	70.6s
4	Johnston, Roger, How, Hansen	73.0s
5	Lawson, Johnston, Forsberg, McKinlay	72.6s
6	Geran, Briggs, Craven, Hansen	72.0s
7	Sormander, Soderman, Roger, Hofmeister (f)	72.6s
8	Fundin, How, White, Williams	72.0s
9	McKinlay, How, Geran, Soderman	72.4s
10	Craven, Roger, Lawson, White	72.0s
11	Sormander, Hansen, Williams, Forsberg	72.4s
12	Briggs, Fundin, Johnson, Hofmeister	71.8s
13	McKinlay, Hansen, White, Hofmeister	71.8s
14	Soderman, Craven, Johnston, Williams	72.0s
*15	Briggs, Lawson, Sormander, How (f/exc)	72.2s
16	Fundin, Roger, Geran, Forsberg (f)	72.6s
17	Briggs, McKinlay, Roger, Williams	72.4s
18	Craven, How, Forsberg, Hofmeister	72.2s
19	Sormander, Johnston, Geran, White	72.6s
20	Fundin, Lawson, Soderman, Hansen	74.6s
21	Briggs beat Fundin in run-off for 1st place	no time
22	Craven beat Lawson and Sormander in run-off for 3rd place	no time

The forceful style of Barry Briggs carried him to his first world title in 1957.

Ove Fundin, Barry Briggs and Peter Craven. Ken McKinlay was also fancied after his performance in 1956.

However, the first race immediately dispelled McKinlay's hopes when he finished last behind Fundin, Craven and Sormander. Aub Lawson showed his experience by winning heats two and five, while Briggs took heat three.

The next surprise came in heat six when Australian Jack Geran outrode both Briggs and Craven. Swedes Sormander and Fundin took heats seven and eight respectively, and after two pointless outings McKinlay switched machines to win heat nine. Craven and Sormander won heats 10 and 11, but a crucial race was to be heat 12, when Briggs and Fundin met. After a tight race Briggs came out on top, leaving himself and Fundin on eight points after three rides each, with Lawson and Sormander on seven, and Craven and Ron Johnston on six.

McKinlay won heat 13 in a fast time, but by now his effort could not affect the leading scorers. Craven lost a vital point when he was beaten by Peo Soderman in heat 14, and Briggs and Lawson put paid to Sormander's hopes in the next race. Fundin consolidated his position with another win in heat 16, and after all riders had had four outings it was clear that the title would be fought out between the Swede and Briggs.

Briggs made his challenge clear with a win over McKinlay in the 17th race, although it was by no means an easy task as the Scot had now recovered his best form — he might well have been a serious contender if he could have produced this kind of fire in his opening rides. Craven won his last ride in heat 18,

and Sormander produced another victory in the penultimate race.

Fundin had to win the last race to equal Briggs' score, and made no mistake in leading home Lawson. This left the stage set for a dramatic climax, with run-offs being necessary to decide all three places on the rostrum.

The title decider proved to be controversial, when Fundin's plans went drastically wrong. He gated first but appeared to want to ride a tactical race, concentrating on keeping Briggs at bay. But on the second lap Briggs forced an opening and drove through, and when Fundin tried to hit back he lost control momentarily, his speeding bike hit the fence, and he went down and out. No blame for the incident could be aimed at Briggs, even though some of the crowd gave him a hard time.

Craven won the next run-off with a start-to-finish victory, earning the £150 for third place overall and the traditional tractor ride around the stadium along with Briggs and runner-up Fundin. Lawson and Sormander had had no challenge to offer Craven in this final race.

The thrust from West German Josef Hofmeister and Norwegian Aage Hansen had been almost non-existent, and 1952 finalist Dan Forsberg was also disappointing. Ian Williams made his Wembley debut, and set a record by becoming the third brother from the famous Welsh family to contest a world final. Oddly enough, the feat was almost equalled on this very same night when Bob Roger rode and scored eight points — brother Cyril had also ridden at Wembley, but the third member of the clan, Bert, had qualified in 1952 but was unable to take his place because of injury.

Sweden's Rune Sormander scored a strong 11 points.

1958
Unbeaten Briggs keeps the crown

FOUR BRITISH semi-finals were raced this year at Belle Vue, Wimbledon, Southampton, and Leicester, with the top 11 riders proceeding to Wembley. A European final was held in Warsaw, the location marking the improvement of Eastern European riders, but the five qualifiers who won through consisted of four Swedes and a West German. The European final also provided the second reserve for the world final, this being another Swede, Peo Soderman.

With the demise of the *Sunday Dispatch* newspaper, a new sponsor had been found in the form of the *Sunday Pictorial*. The paper generously donated a new trophy which was competed for right up to 1977.

Pre-Wembley favourites were Ove Fundin and Barry Briggs, the reigning champion. Briggs was seeded direct to the final, while Fundin had scored a maximum in the European final. However, Ken McKinlay and Peter Craven were also on hot form, each having scored 27 points out of a possible 30 in the British

Above: Barry Briggs receives the champion's trophy from the land and water speed record holder, the late Donald Campbell. This was the famous 'winged wheel' Sunday Pictorial trophy, competed for up to 1977.

Right: Aub Lawson, a veteran campaigner in ten world finals, achieved his best result in 1958 with third place.

qualifiers. A famous name missing from the contenders was that of Jack Young, who had walked out of his second semi-final in protest at being excluded from a race for allegedly causing a crash, thus forfeiting any chance of appearing at Wembley.

In sparkling form, Briggs won the first heat from Craven and Aub Lawson, while Olle Nygren took the second race. Ronnie Moore, who had come out of retirement this season, won heat three from McKinlay, and Fundin achieved the tough feat of winning heats four and five to demonstrate to Briggs that he was out for revenge for his defeat of the previous year.

Lawson spoiled Moore's hopes in the sixth heat, and in the seventh Craven relegated McKinlay to another second place. Briggs produced another scintillating ride in heat eight, besting Rune Sormander with Jack Geran — who had beaten Briggs in a heat race in the 1957 final — humbled into third place. McKinlay won heat nine from a persistent Gerry Hussey, and in the next race Lawson spoiled Nygren's hopes. So at the half-way stage it looked like a confrontation for the championship between Fundin and Briggs once again, with Craven holding an outside chance.

The little Englishman's fate was sealed in the next race, however, when he bowed out with machine trouble. Then the two main contenders met in heat 12, and with Ron Johnston and Moore also on the line it had the makings of an exciting contest. Fundin made the gate, chased by Johnston, but 'Briggo' was in no mood to play a waiting game and took them both from the back in the inimitable daredevil fashion that has not always endeared him to speedway purists. With three more points and a win over his greatest rival under his belt, Briggs must have been feeling in fine form at this stage, while Moore had finished last and was clearly out of contention for the major honours among the top three.

Johnston was out again in the next race and won it, but Fundin was given a race to remember in heat 14 when McKinlay exerted pressure and Lawson stayed close behind to take advantage of any slips made by the leading duo. Craven showed his class by taking heat 15 from Nygren and Moore, and when Briggs won heat 16 all riders had had four outings. The score chart showed that Briggs was unbeaten so far, but Fundin had dropped only one point, while McKinlay and Nygren had dropped three points, and Lawson and Craven had missed four.

Lawson placed himself in a strong position by winning his last ride in heat 18, and to the delight of the crowd, Craven put one over Fundin in heat 19 in a classic performance.

Briggs could afford to drop a point in heat 20 and still take the championship, but McKinlay had to win if he was to make third place on the rostrum. If Briggs won, a run-off for third place would be required between McKinlay, Craven and Lawson. From the tapes Briggs streamed away, and McKinlay was never in the hunt - perhaps he remembered all too well the disastrous occasion in 1956 when he fell in his last race while still holding a chance of becoming world champion. At least by riding easily behind Briggs in this race he would be assured of a place in the run-off for third position overall.

The run-off, however, became an anti-climax when Lawson streaked from the gate, and 'Hurri-Ken' dropped his bike while in too much of a hurry, and Craven repeated the feat when he took up the challenge. Lawson finished alone, to pick up the third-placed man's £100 cheque.

Briggs's victory over Fundin made him the champion of the world for a second time, and in successive years. The first achievement equalled previous performances by Jack Young and Freddie Williams, while on the second count he repeated Young's efforts in winning consecutive championships in 1951 and 1952.

Even though he had been runner-up at the European Final in Warsaw just a few weeks previously, Josef Hofmeister again failed to come to terms with the Wembley track.

Score Chart

								Total
1	Barry Briggs	New Zealand	3	3	3	3	3	15
2	Ove Fundin	Sweden	3	3	2	3	2	13
3	Aub Lawson	Australia	1	3	3	1	3	11
4	Peter Craven	England	2	3	ef	3	3	11
	Ken McKinlay	Scotland	2	2	3	2	2	11
6	Olle Nygren	Sweden	3	2	2	2	0	9
	Ronnie Moore	New Zealand	3	2	0	1	3	9
8	Ron Johnston	New Zealand	1	1	1	3	2	8
9	Gerald Hussey	England	2	0	2	2	1	7
	Ron How	England	1	1	2	2	1	7
11	Mike Broadbanks	England	2	0	1	0	2	5
	Peter Moore	Australia	f	1	3	1	0	5
13	Rune Sormander	Sweden	0	2	0	1	1	4
14	Jack Geran	Australia	f	1	1	0	1	3
15	Josef Hofmeister	W Germany	1	0	0	1	0	2
16	Joel Jansson	Sweden	0	0	0	0	0	0
	Brian Crutcher (res)	England			(did not ride)			
	Peo Soderman (res)	Sweden			(did not ride)			

Heat-by-heat

		Time
1	Briggs, Craven, Lawson, Jansson	74.2s
2	Nygren, Hussey, Johnston, Geran (f)	74.8s
3	R Moore, McKinlay, Hofmeister, P Moore (f)	74.4s
4	Fundin, Broadbanks, How, Sormander	74.6s
5	Fundin, Nygren, P Moore, Jansson	74.4s
6	Lawson, R Moore, How, Hussey	74.0s
7	Craven, McKinlay, Johnston, Broadbanks	73.6s
8	Briggs, Sormander, Geran, Hofmeister	74.0s
9	McKinlay, Hussey, Sormander, Jansson	74.6s
10	Lawson, Nygren, Broadbanks, Hofmeister	74.6s
11	P Moore, How, Geran, Craven (ef)	74.0s
12	Briggs, Fundin, Johnston, R Moore	73.4s
13	Johnston, How, Hofmeister, Jansson	75.2s
14	Fundin, McKinlay, Lawson, Geran	74.0s
15	Craven, Nygren, R Moore, Sormander	74.4s
16	Briggs, Hussey, P Moore, Broadbanks	73.6s
17	R Moore, Broadbanks, Geran, Jansson	75.6s
18	Lawson, Johnston, Sormander, P Moore	74.8s
19	Craven, Fundin, Hussey, Hofmeister	74.0s
20	Briggs, McKinlay, How, Nygren	74.6s
21	Lawson beat Craven and McKinlay (f) in run-off for 3rd place	

1959
Ronnie Moore all the way

THE ESTABLISHED pattern for qualifying rounds was repeated this year. From the Continental Final at Munich and the Nordic Final at Turku in Finland, the top eight riders from each event went forward to the Grand European Final at Gothenburg, Sweden, in July, from which Ove Fundin emerged as European title holder.

The British semi-finals at Wimbledon, Southampton, Norwich and Belle Vue produced a new top qualifier in Australian Peter Moore - no relation to Kiwi Ronnie Moore - who scored 27 out of a possible 30 points. One point behind were Peter Craven and Brian Crutcher. The top nine from the British qualifiers went to Wembley where they were joined by Europe's top six, plus reigning champion Barry Briggs, who was seeded direct to Wembley.

Could Briggs make it a hat-trick of wins in successive years? That was the obvious question for 1959. Briggs's chances, however, were less than they might have been, for he had remained in New Zealand for most of the season while in dispute with the Wimbledon management. He returned to Britain only to defend his world title, and these circumstances were to have a notable effect on events at Wembley.

An East European, Pole Mieczyslaw Polukard — rapidly nicknamed 'Mike' — appeared in a world final for the first time. The only other newcomers were the young Swede Arne Carlsson and the Polish reserve, Florian Kapala, who was not called on to ride. Favourites for the title were Ove Fundin, Craven, the persistent Crutcher, and Ronnie Moore. Briggs's absence from competitive league racing made him something of an unknown quantity, even though he was the reigning champion.

Crutcher looked good in the first heat when he stormed to a win over Geoff Mardon. Craven caused British hopes to drop by starting badly in the second heat and remaining last, as Aub Lawson won the race from Rune Sormander. Briggs showed that he had lost none of his ability by taking heat three from the impressive Carlsson. Then Ronnie Moore and Fundin met in heat four, and the New Zealander led from the gate, never looking like being beaten. Moore had an even easier victory in heat five from Polukard, who kept Sormander at bay.

A 13-point total kept Ove Fundin in the top three for his fourth consecutive final.

Sweden's Olle Nygren scored 11 points in the 1959 final.

Heat six was the most crucial race so far, pitching together Lawson, Briggs, Fundin and Englishman George White. Lawson made a flier from the gate, while Fundin was caught sleeping and entered the first turn in last position. But on the first lap he passed White and Briggs, and then levelled with Lawson as they entered the final lap. But the crafty Lawson took his Norwich team-mate out to the fence and won a superb race, while Briggo's third place cost him two points.

Another victim of a poor start was Craven in heat seven, leaving Carlsson to show his class with a victory over Crutcher. Craven just made it into third place by passing Cyril Roger on the last bend. Heat nine brought a tussle between Lawson and Nygren, and a show of high-tension temper. Nygren won from Lawson and Carlsson, and after the race Lawson was warned by the referee and also healthily booed by the crowd. But it was all entertaining stuff, and just what speedway is about.

Fundin beat Crutcher in heat 11 to record his first win of the night, and then heat 12 matched together three great riders, Ronnie Moore, Briggs and Craven. Wild riding by Craven gave Moore the chance to break away in front, and after Briggs had won a battle with Geoff Mardon at the back he almost caught Craven on the line. With all riders now having had three rides, Moore looked a potential champion with an unbeaten nine points. Lawson still had eight, Fundin and Crutcher were on seven, while Nygren had dropped three points and defending champion Briggs had missed four.

After another bad start, Fundin managed to beat Craven in the 13th race, and Moore took the 14th to keep his chances on the boil. Briggs grabbed back some points by beating Nygren in heat 15, when Crutcher finished third and knew that his chance of the big money had disappeared. The crowd showed their delight when Josef Hofmeister surprisingly beat Lawson in heat 16, and Briggo won his last outing in the 17th.

Nygren beat Craven in heat 18, and Moore now needed only a second place from his final ride in heat 19 to take the title. He went one better by easily beating Crutcher and Lawson, inheriting the world championship for the second time. He had achieved it with an unbeaten run.

Fundin needed a second place from his last ride in heat 20 to be sure of second place overall — if he finished third he would join Lawson, Nygren and Briggs in a run-off to decide the placings behind Moore. But Fundin made no mistake, finishing second overall on 13 points. The run-off for third place saw all three riders hit the first bend together, but Briggs and Nygren came out ahead of Lawson. Nygren eased ahead, but Briggs drove under him on the second lap, without success. On the third lap he tried an outside line, still without getting by, but a final huge handful of throttle on the last turn gave Briggs the race win and third place in the championship. Still being booed, the out-of-favour Lawson trailed in third, to take fifth place overall behind Nygren.

George White scored seven points in the last of his two final appearances.

Score Chart

								Total
1 Ronnie Moore	New Zealand	3	3	3	3	3		15
2 Ove Fundin	Sweden	2	2	3	3	3		13
3 Barry Briggs	New Zealand	3	1	1	3	3		11
4 Olle Nygren	Sweden	1	2	3	2	3		11
Aub Lawson	Australia	3	3	2	2	1		11
6 Brian Crutcher	England	3	2	2	1	2		10
7 Arne Carlsson	Sweden	2	3	1	1	1		8
8 Peter Craven	England	0	1	2	2	2		7
George White	England	1	0	3	2	1		7
10 Geoff Mardon	New Zealand	2	3	0	1	ef		6
Rune Sormander	Sweden	2	1	1	0	2		6
12 Mieczyslaw Polukard	Poland	0	2	0	1	2		5
13 Josef Hofmeister	W Germany	0	ef	1	3	f/e		4
14 Ron How	England	1	1	ef	ef	1		3
Peter Moore	Australia	1	0	2	0	0		3
16 Cyril Roger	England	0	0	0	0	0		0
Ken McKinlay (res)	Scotland	(did not ride)						
Florian Kapala (res)	Poland	(did not ride)						

Heat-by-Heat

		Time
1	Crutcher, Mardon, White, Polukard	71.6s
2	Lawson, Sormander, How, Craven	71.8s
3	Briggs, Carlsson, P Moore, Hofmeister	71.4s
4	R Moore, Fundin, Nygren, Roger	71.6s
5	R Moore, Polukard, Sormander, Hofmeister (ef)	71.4s
6	Lawson, Fundin, Briggs, White	72.0s
7	Carlsson, Crutcher, Craven, Roger	71.6s
8	Mardon, Nygren, How, P Moore	71.4s
9	Nygren, Lawson, Carlsson, Polukard	72.6s
10	White, P Moore, Sormander, Roger	72.0s
11	Fundin, Crutcher, Hofmeister, How (ef)	72.2s
12	R Moore, Craven, Briggs, Mardon	71.6s
13	Fundin, Craven, Polukard, P Moore	71.8s
14	R Moore, White, Carlsson, How (ef)	72.2s
15	Briggs, Nygren, Crutcher, Sormander	71.6s
16	Hofmeister, Lawson, Mardon, Roger	72.4s
17	Briggs, Polukard, How, Roger	71.6s
18	Nygren, Craven, White, Hofmeister (f/exc)	72.4s
19	R Moore, Crutcher, Lawson, P Moore	72.4s
20	Fundin, Sormander, Carlsson, Mardon (ef)	74.0s
21	Briggs beat Nygren and Lawson in run-off for 3rd place	72.6s

1960
Battle of the giants

Poland's Marian Kaiser (left) won the 1960 European championship, with Stefan Kwoczala in third place.

AFTER SPEEDWAY'S slump in popularity in the fifties, 1960 brought the formation of the Provincial League, which in effect replaced Divisions Two and Three of more popular times. Qualifying procedures were extended to these new tracks, nine rounds being staged, with the top 20 scorers moving forward to eliminators on the ten National League, or Division One, ovals. From this stage the top 24 scorers contested the semi-finals at Wimbledon, Southampton, Coventry, and Belle Vue. Peter Craven headed the semi-final scorers with an unbeaten run of 30 points, followed by Ron How and Ken McKinlay on 28. The next six most successful riders joined them at Wembley together with the seeded world champion Ronnie Moore, and the six leading riders from the Continental Final at Wroclaw in Poland. From this latter meeting Poland's Marian Kaiser emerged as European champion, from Ove Fundin and Stefan Kwoczala. In fourth place, Henryk Zyto underlined the fact that Poland was at last recognised as a serious force in speedway.

The final itself was one of the most eventful to date, a three-way run-off being necessary to settle the top three placings. Oddly enough, on the way to the run-off the racing thrills were in short supply, with only one or two heats being the exception.

Fundin won heat one from Chum Taylor, with Jack Young a poor third. In great form, Craven took the next heat from Barry Briggs and Aub Lawson, and in the

Ronnie Moore (left) and Bjorn Knutsson clash in a qualifying round. Knutsson failed to reach the final, but his best years were to start in 1961.

third Ronnie Moore won in the fastest time of the night from Peter Moore, with McKinlay a poor last behind Zyto. After Ron Johnston had won heat four, all the big guns had been out and only Briggs had dropped a point.

Briggs received a further blow in the next race, when both McKinlay and Johnston showed him the line home. Fundin won again in the sixth heat, but surprise package Peter Moore made Craven work hard for his success in heat seven. Ronnie Moore beat Young in heat eight, and Peter Moore confirmed he was a serious contender for the title with a fine win in the ninth.

Heat 10 brought together a battle of the giants, with Ronnie Moore, Fundin and Briggs lining up, together with Bryan Elliott. Moore led all the way from Fundin, but Briggs looked out of touch. In heat 11 Kwoczala beat his Leicester team-mate McKinlay, and in heat 12 Craven won from his Belle Vue partner Johnston, with Young third. Craven was out again in the next heat, and put in a great race to beat the determined Ronnie Moore.

Fundin put paid to the aspirations of Peter Moore and Johnston in heat 14, and Briggs, at last riding in typical form, won the 15th. When Josef Hofmeister beat Young and McKinlay in heat 16, all riders had had four outings, and Craven was the only unbeaten man on 12 points. Moore and Fundin each had 11, while Peter Moore was still challenging on nine. The crowd had to wait until heat 18 before Craven and Fundin were to meet.

'Chum' Taylor won heat 17 from reserve Bob Andrews, who had replaced Elliott, unfortunately excluded under the two minute rule. But the stadium's attention was already on the crucial next race, which matched Craven against Fundin, McKinlay and Rune Sormander. Depending on the result, Craven could clinch the title, or a three-man run-off would be necessary.

Fundin led from the gate, pursued by Craven and McKinlay. Craven tried to get round the Swede but merely found himself filled in with flying shale from the leader. Meanwhile Sormander had passed McKinlay, but all eyes were on Craven as he tried again, and took a big handful of throttle round the outside line in an attempt to clinch the title on the final turn. But instead he hit a pothole in the track surface, the force of the impact pitching him forward on to the handlebars. Craven stayed on and retained second place, but he was helped off his machine at the pits and was obviously in great pain.

Ronnie Moore needed to win the 19th heat to ensure his place in the triple run-off. This he did, though not without harassment from Hofmeister early in the race until the German fell, leaving Johnston to take second place. Peter Moore won heat 20 from Briggs, to claim fourth place overall. A rare sight in this race was the spectacle of the immaculate Jack Young sliding off.

The run-off to decide the destiny of the world championship in a single race called together Craven, Fundin and Ronnie Moore. From the inside starting berth, Craven made a poor gate and followed Fundin and Moore into the first turn. Moore drove round the fence, cutting to the inside on the exit from the bend in an attempt to pass Fundin. But the Swede kept Moore out, and pulled way to join the elite club of double world champions, Young, Freddie Williams and Briggs being the only other members. Meanwhile Moore held off Craven's challenge for second place in both the run-off and the championship. It's possible that Craven's earlier incident had affected his form in the run-off, but as the perennial adage goes, 'That's speedway'.

Eric Williams, who returned to New Zealand for domestic reasons, and the injured Ron How were unable to take their places among the Wembley participants, and their positions were taken by reserves Taylor and Elliott.

Score Chart

								Total
1 Ove Fundin	Sweden	3	3	2	3	3	14
2 Ronnie Moore	New Zealand	3	3	3	2	3	14
3 Peter Craven	England	3	3	3	3	2	14
4 Peter Moore	Australia	2	2	3	2	3	12
5 Ron Johnston	New Zealand	3	2	2	1	2	10
6 Barry Briggs	New Zealand	2	1	1	3	2	9
7 Stefan Kwoczala	Poland	1	2	3	1	1	8
8 Josef Hofmeister	W Germany	0	0	2	3	1	6
Ken McKinlay	Scotland	0	3	2	1	0	6
Jack Young	Australia	1	2	1	2	f	6
11 Rune Sormander	Sweden	2	0	1	1	1	5
Chum Taylor	Australia	2	0	0	0	3	5
13 Aub Lawson	Australia	1	1	1	0	1	4
Henryk Zyto	Poland	1	1	0	2	0	4
15 Marian Kaiser	Poland	0	1	0	0	0	1
16 Bryan Elliott	England	0	ef	ef	0	ns	0
Bob Andrews (res)	England					2	2
Mieczyslaw Polukard (res)	Poland	(did not ride)					

NB: Ron How (England) and Eric Williams (Wales) both qualified but were unable to ride. Their places were taken by Taylor and Elliott.

Heat-by-Heat

		Time
1	Fundin, Taylor, Young, Kaiser	69.6s
2	Craven, Briggs, Lawson, Hofmeister	68.8s
3	R Moore, P Moore, Zyto, McKinlay	69.6s
4	Johnston, Sormander, Kwoczala, Elliott	71.0s
5	McKinlay, Johnston, Briggs, Taylor	70.4s
6	Fundin, Kwoczala, Zyto, Hofmeister	70.0s
7	Craven, P Moore, Kaiser, Elliott (ef)	69.6s
8	R Moore, Young, Lawson, Sormander	70.8s
9	P Moore, Hofmeister, Sormander, Taylor	71.4s
10	R Moore, Fundin, Briggs, Elliott (ef)	69.6s
11	Kwoczala, McKinlay, Lawson, Kaiser	71.4s
12	Craven, Johnston, Young, Zyto	71.0s
13	Craven, R Moore, Kwoczala, Taylor	69.4s
14	Fundin, P Moore, Johnston, Lawson	70.8s
15	Briggs, Zyto, Sormander, Kaiser	70.6s
16	Hofmeister, Young, McKinlay, Elliott	71.8s
17	Taylor, Andrews, Lawson, Zyto	70.8s
18	Fundin, Craven, Sormander, McKinlay	69.8s
19	R Moore, Johnston, Hofmeister, Kaiser	70.8s
20	P Moore, Briggs, Kwoczala, Young (f)	71.6s
21	Fundin beat R Moore and Craven in run-off to decide the first three places.	70.6s

1961

The move from Wembley to Sweden

Score Chart

								Total
1 Ove Fundin	Sweden	3	3	3	3	2		14
2 Bjorn Knutsson	Sweden	3	3	3	f	3		12
3 Gote Nordin	Sweden	2	2	2	3	3		12
4 Barry Briggs	New Zealand	1	3	3	2	3		12
5 Bob Andrews	England	2	2	2	1	3		10
Ronnie Moore	New Zealand	3	1	2	2	2		10
7 Florian Kapala	Poland	0	2	2	3	1		8
8 Ron How	England	2	3	1	1	0		7
Rune Sormander	Sweden	2	1	0	3	1		7
10 Peter Craven	England	f	2	3	0	1		6
11 Ken McKinlay	Scotland	3	f/r	1	1	ef		5
12 Cyril Maidment	England	1	0	1	2	0		4
Igor Plechanov	USSR	1	0	1	0	2		4
14 Ray Cresp	Australia	f	1	0	f	2		3
Stanislaw Tkocz	Poland	0	0	0	2	1		3
16 Mike Broadbanks	England	0	1	0	1	0		2
Jack Young (res)	Australia	(did not ride)						
Leif Larsson (res)	Sweden	(did not ride)						

Heat-by-Heat

		Time
1	Knutsson, Andrews, Plechanov, Kapala	77.5s
2	Fundin, Sormander, Cresp (f), Craven (f)	79.1s
3	McKinlay, How, Maidment, Tkocz	79.3s
4	Moore, Nordin, Briggs, Broadbanks	78.7s
5	How, Nordin, Cresp, Plechanov	80.0s
6	Fundin, Andrews, Broadbanks, McKinlay (f/re)	79.2s
7	Briggs, Kapala, Sormander, Tkocz	79.8s
8	Knutsson, Craven, Moore, Maidment	78.1s
9	Fundin, Moore, Plechanov, Tkocz	78.9s
10	Briggs, Andrews, Maidment, Cresp	78.7s
11	Craven, Kapala, How, Broadbanks	79.0s
12	Knutsson, Nordin, McKinlay, Sormander	78.2s
13	Sormander, Maidment, Broadbanks, Plechanov	80.0s
14	Nordin, Tkocz, Andrews, Craven	79.8s
15	Kapala, Moore, McKinlay, Cresp (f)	79.0s
16	Fundin, Briggs, How, Knutsson (f)	79.4s
17	Briggs, Plechanov, Craven, McKinlay (ef)	79.7s
18	Andrews, Moore, Sormander, How	79.7s
19	Nordin, Fundin, Kapala, Maidment	79.6s
20	Knutsson, Cresp, Tkocz, Broadbanks	79.7s
21	Knutsson beat Nordin and Briggs to decide 2nd, 3rd and 4th places	78.7s

SPEEDWAY HISTORY was made this season, when for the first time the world final was held outside the UK. Sweden had been pressing to stage the event as their riders had performed so well in recent years — they had twice had a world champion in Ove Fundin. So, for 1961, the final was run on the Malmo track.

British qualifying rounds followed the pattern of the previous year, with the Provincial League eliminators offering Maurice Mattingley as top scorer with 29 points out of 30. Peter Craven led the way on the National League cricuits, with an unbeaten 30 points. From the semi-finals at Wimbledon, Southampton, Belle Vue and Norwich, Barry Briggs and Ronnie Moore were top scorers on 29 points each, and headed the qualifiers into the British Final at Wembley on 2 September. The top nine riders went forward to Malmo, Briggs winning the British Final with a 15-point maximum from Craven, who scored 14.

Meanwhile, the Scandinavian round was being raced across the North Sea, and the Continental rounds were fought out in central Europe. Fundin won the Scandinavian championship, and Pole Florian Kapala was best in the Continental Final. The top eight riders from each meeting progressed to the European Final in Austria, where Ove Fundin was unbeaten with 15 points, and accompanied the next six highest scorers to Malmo.

Before a 25,000 crowd in the compact Swedish stadium, Bjorn Knutsson won the first heat in what proved to be the fastest time of the meeting. Heat two turned into an anti-climax, when the anticipated tussle between Fundin and Craven failed to materialise. Australian Ray Cresp fell, and in laying down his machine to avoid the stricken rider, Craven damaged a knee and was unable to remount. Ken McKinlay raised British hopes with a fine win in heat three, and Moore beat both Swede Gote Nordin and Briggs in the fourth race. While this was happening, the starting gate had ceased to operate, and a strand of strong elastic was used to good effect.

Ron How won again for Britain in the fifth heat, but Fundin took his second victory of the meeting in the next race. Briggs put it all together to win heat eight from Kapala, who was back on form after trailing in last in his first outing. Craven looked uncomfortable in heat eight when he was beaten by Knutsson, and in the ninth Fundin bested Moore, who never let the reigning champion relax. Briggs took heat 10, Craven headed a hard-riding Kapala in the 11th, and top Swedes Knutsson and Nordin battled it out in heat 12. With all riders now having completed three rides, Fundin and Knutsson were unbeaten on nine points each, and Briggs followed them on seven.

Heat 14 was probably the most exciting of the night, when Nordin won a hectic battle from Pole Stanislaw Tkocz. Craven was last in this race, and was obviously suffering discomfort from his earlier contact with the track. The ever-improving Kapala showed Moore and McKinlay home in heat 15, which led up to probably the most crucial race of the night in heat 16. Fundin, Knutsson and Briggs lined up, with How in a position to act as spoiler to any of the big three. Fundin led from

Under the Malmo lights, Ove Fundin hurls his machine to a popular home victory.

the gate, but Knutsson went sprawling on the track when he made a big effort around the outside and found too much grip. While Knutsson was left to reflect that his fall could have cost him the title, Briggs and How followed Fundin home. Heat 17 saw Briggs winning from Russian Igor Plechanov and a subdued Craven, and Bob Andrews took the next race from Moore.

Fundin needed only a third place from heat 19 to become the first rider to win the world championship three times. And despite rearing at the gate, he achieved his aim by notching a second place behind Nordin. By winning the final heat with a faultless ride, Knutsson forced a run-off between himself, Nordin and Briggs for the second, third and fourth places. And with another flawless performance Knutsson gained the runner-up spot, while Nordin seemed content to keep Briggs behind him to make it a Swedish 1-2-3 in the overall standings. This was the first time since England's onslaught in 1949 that a single nation had filled the first three places in the World Speedway Championship, and only the third time in the entire history of the series that this had happened — America was the other victorious country, back in 1937.

Ex-champion Jack Young put up with the indignity of being reserve for this meeting, but did not have to ride. Neither did Swede Leif Larsson, who replaced the original European reserve, the injured Josef Hofmeister.

Gote Nordin (right) and Bjorn Knutsson helped Sweden to a 1-2-3 success in 1961.

1962
The pocket rocket scores again

WHEN THE world final returned to Wembley in 1962, British hopes were high for a home win after the Swedish domination of the previous year. British qualifying rounds followed the 1961 pattern, with top scorers from the Provincial League events graduating to National League tracks, which fed the best performers to semi-finals at Wimbledon, Southampton, Oxford, and Norwich.

Confirming speedway's genuine international status, Nordic rounds were staged in Sweden, Finland, Denmark, and Norway, and Continental events were held in Austria, Yugoslavia, and Russia. The top eight riders from the Nordic Final in Denmark and the Continental Final in Warsaw met in the European Final at Oslo, which sent eight riders to Wembley to ride against the top eight Britons.

Most European countries that staged speedway

World champion after a seven-year gap, Peter Craven keeps Barry Briggs in the background.

were represented in the 65,000 crowd at Wembley. The track was in first class condition for the meeting, and this was no doubt a contributory factor in persuading reigning world champion Ove Fundin to ride. He arrived at the stadium on crutches, with a leg in plaster and a protective wire cage on a knee, all as a result of a recent track accident.

Heat one saw Ronnie Moore jet from the gate, while Barry Briggs made an atrocious start and failed to catch Gote Nordin in second place. Bjorn Knutsson easily won the second race, and the injured Fundin miraculously took the third despite pressure from Ron How. Heat four was re-run after Rune Sormander fell, and in the restart the unperturbed Swede led from the gate until Peter Craven, riding at his best, got by on the second lap to win in a very fast time. Bob Andrews dented the hopes of the more fancied Nordin and

Score Chart

							Total
1 Peter Craven	England	3	2	3	3	3	14
2 Barry Briggs	New Zealand	1	3	3	3	3	13
3 Ove Fundin	Sweden	3	0	1	3	3	10
4 Bjorn Knutsson	Sweden	3	1	ef	3	3	10
5 Ken McKinlay	Scotland	2	2	3	2	f	9
Ronnie Moore	New Zealand	3	3	ef	2	1	9
Bob Andrews	England	0	3	2	2	2	9
Gote Nordin	Sweden	2	2	2	1	2	9
9 Soren Sjosten	Sweden	0	3	2	1	2	8
10 Igor Plechanov	USSR	1	1	3	1	1	7
Rune Sormander	Sweden	2	1	0	2	2	7
12 Ron How	England	2	2	2	0	0	6
13 Arne Carlsson	Sweden	0	1	1	0	0	2
Mike Broadbanks	England	1	ef	0	0	1	2
Ron Mountford	England	0	1	1	0	0	2
Pawel Waloszek	Poland	1	0	1	0	0	2
Nigel Boocock (res)	England	(did not ride)					
Henryk Zyto (res)	Poland	(did not ride)					

Heat-by-heat

		Time
1	Moore, Nordin, Briggs, Sjosten	71.6s
2	Knutsson, McKinlay, Waloszek, Mountford	71.2s
3	Fundin, How, Plechanov, Andrews	70.8s
4	Craven, Sormander, Broadbanks, Carlsson	69.6s
5	Andrews, Nordin, Sormander, Waloszek	71.0s
6	Briggs, Craven, Knutsson, Fundin	70.4s
7	Moore, McKinlay, Plechanov, Broadbanks (ef)	71.4s
8	Sjosten, How, Mountford, Carlsson	70.8s
9	Plechanov, Nordin, Carlsson, Knutsson (ef)	71.2s
10	Briggs, How, Waloszek, Broadbanks	71.0s
11	Craven, Andrews, Mountford, Moore	69.2s
12	McKinlay, Sjosten, Fundin, Sormander	70.2s
13	Craven, McKinlay, Nordin, How	70.0s
14	Briggs, Sormander, Plechanov, Mountford	71.4s
15	Fundin, Moore, Carlsson, Waloszek	70.8s
16	Knutsson, Andrews, Sjosten, Broadbanks	70.4s
17	Fundin, Nordin, Broadbanks, Mountford	71.6s
18	Briggs, Andrews, Carlsson, McKinlay (f)	71.6s
19	Knutsson, Sormander, Moore, How	70.2s
20	Craven, Sjosten, Plechanov, Waloszek	71.0s
21	Fundin beat Knutsson (f) in run-off for 3rd place	69.4s

Sormander in heat five, while Pole Pawel Waloszek looked out of touch at the back.

Heat six was the race of the night, bringing together four of speedway's super-stars in Briggs, Knutsson, Craven and Fundin. Briggs left the gate almost as if airborne, Knutsson followed him, but Craven was a fraction late in getting away and Fundin was even slower. The thrills came from Craven as he bustled past Knutsson and gave chase to Briggo. But there was no way of getting past the lanky New Zealander, and Craven had to settle for a dropped point. To make matters worse for the English hope, Ronnie Moore won the seventh heat from Ken McKinlay, to make himself the only unbeaten rider after each man had had two outings.

Knutsson suffered tragedy in heat nine when he retired with engine trouble, although he probably would not have caught the flying Russian Igor Plechanov, who won from Nordin. Briggs kept in the running by winning heat 10, but there was drama in the next race. Craven pulled back into contention by winning in the fastest time of the night, but Moore was handicapped by a loose fuel tank, finishing last and losing his grip on the title.

Heat 12 saw the closest finish of the meeting with McKinlay just getting the verdict from the fiery little Swede, Soren Sjosten. Handicapped by his injuries, Fundin finished third and bid farewell to his slender chances of retaining his championship. McKinlay was out again in the next heat, and started like a rocket, but Craven rode around him and emerged as favourite to take over Fundin's title.

The crowd saw Briggs's determination displayed to the full when he passed Plechanov to win heat 14, and Sormander followed him through the gap to push the Russian back into third place. Moore was beaten by a gallant Fundin in heat 15, and Knutsson took the 16th heat in his finest style. With all riders now having completed four races, Craven led the field with 11 points, Briggs was close on 10, McKinlay had nine and Moore eight.

Heat 17 went to the plucky Fundin, who was suddenly back in with a chance of a ride on the tractor. Heat 18 saw sensational happenings when McKinlay sped from the gate and led Briggs a merry dance until the former's throttle jammed open. The Scot was thrown from his machine, which careered along the track for 20 yards while Briggs won and gave himself a challenging 13-point total for the night.

Heat 19 saw Moore lose his chance of a placing in the top three when he finished third to Knutsson and Sormander. This now left Craven to win the final heat if he wanted to become world champion for the second time. He lined up against Plechanov, Sjosten and Waloszek, but Craven made the gate and won as he pleased. England had a world champion again for the first time since Craven's previous victory in 1955.

Fundin led the run-off for third place all the way from Knutsson, who climaxed a desperate last bend effort by spinning round, crossing the inner edge of the track and falling.

1963 Fundin conquers injuries

WHILE QUALIFYING rounds for the 1963 final were run on similar lines to the previous two seasons, Wembley's big night proved to be one of the most dramatic ever partly because Ove Fundin was handicapped for the second consecutive year by injuries. This time he was suffering from a damaged leg and shoulder.

The 62,000 crowd was immediately put in the right mood when England's Nigel Boocock won the first heat in his first ever ride in a world final. Norway's Sverre Harrfeldt chased hard, but could not hold back the determined 'Booey'. Heat two put some of the favourites together, Ronnie Moore, reigning champion Peter Craven, Bjorn Knutsson and Peo Soderman being the starters. Into the first turn Moore led from Soderman and Knutsson, with Craven at the back. But Craven switched from the outside line to the inside to pass Soderman and Knutsson, and by the end of the lap he had ridden under Moore to take a winning lead. Knutsson also followed Craven past Moore, so the battle of the giants was well and truly on.

Controversy arrived as early as heat three, when the hard Russian Boris Samorodov met Barry Briggs, Fundin and Ron How. Fundin led from the gate with a wheelie, and Briggs was close with him. But at the back Samorodov charged into How, unseating him, and the race was stopped. The referee excluded Samorodov from the re-run, but the Russian at first refused to leave the track, and only returned to the pits after he had been heavily booed by the crowd. In the restart Fundin again got away first with Briggs in close attendance. But on the third lap Briggo made a big effort around the outside, only to fall. He remounted to take third place, but now knew that only a superhuman effort could win him the title.

Gote Nordin won the fourth heat from first-time finalist Leo McAuliffe, but the fifth heat brought together the first three race winners, Boocock, Fundin and Nordin. The start was ragged and should really

Sverre Harrfeldt made an impressive world final debut, scoring 10 points.

Score Chart

								Total
1	Ove Fundin	Sweden	3	3	2	3	3	14
2	Bjorn Knutsson	Sweden	2	2	3	3	3	13
3	Barry Briggs	New Zealand	1	3	3	3	2	12
4	Boris Samorodov	USSR	exc	3	3	2	3	11
5	Gote Nordin	Sweden	3	2	3	1	1	10
	Sverre Harrfeldt	Norway	2	2	1	2	3	10
7	Nigel Boocock	England	3	1	1	2	1	8
8	Ron How	England	2	3	f	f	2	7
	Leo McAuliffe	Wales	2	ef	2	3	0	7
10	Peter Craven	England	3	1	f	2	0	6
	Peter Moore	Australia	1	1	1	2	1	6
12	Peo Soderman	Sweden	0	0	2	1	2	5
	Dick Fisher	England	1	1	2	0	1	5
14	Jim Lightfoot	England	ef	2	1	0	1	4
15	Per Tage Svensson	Sweden	1	f	0	0	0	1
	Arne Carlsson	Sweden	0	0	0	1	0	1
	Ron Mountford (res)	England	(did not ride)					
	Tadeuz Teodorowicz (res)	England	(did not ride)					

NB: Antonin Kasper was the qualifying Continental reserve but was unfit. His place was taken by Ron Mountford, Tadeuz Teodorowicz being a naturalised British subject.

Heat-by-Heat

		Time
1	Boocock, Harrfeldt, Fisher, Lightfoot (ef)	70.4s
2	Craven, Knutsson, Moore, Soderman	69.0s
3	Fundin, How, Briggs (f/re), Samorodov (exc)	68.4s
4	Nordin, McAuliffe, Svensson, Carlsson	70.4s
5	Fundin, Nordin, Boocock, Soderman	69.6s
6	How, Lightfoot, Craven (f/re), Svensson (f)	71.8s
7	Samorodov, Harrfeldt, Moore, Carlsson	71.0s
8	Briggs, Knutsson, Fisher, McAuliffe (ef)	69.6s
9	Samorodov, McAuliffe, Boocock, Craven (f)	70.4s
10	Briggs, Soderman, Lightfoot, Carlsson	70.0s
11	Knutsson, Fundin, Harrfeldt, Svensson	69.2s
12	Nordin, Fisher, Moore, How (f)	70.4s
13	Briggs, Boocock, Moore, Svensson	70.2s
14	Knutsson, Samorodov, Nordin, Lightfoot	69.6s
15	McAuliffe, Harrfeldt, Soderman, How (f)	71.6s
16	Fundin, Craven, Carlsson, Fisher	69.8s
17	Knutsson, How, Boocock, Carlsson	70.2s
18	Fundin, Moore, Lightfoot, McAuliffe	69.4s
19	Harrfeldt, Briggs, Nordin, Craven	70.4s
20	Samorodov, Soderman, Fisher, Svensson	71.8s

have been re-run, but Fundin took advantage of the confusion to shoot ahead. Nordin took second place after bouncing off Boocock, and although the Englishman managed to pull back and take third place from Soderman, he must have been wondering why the race was allowed to continue.

Craven had what looked like an easy outing in heat six, but was badly away and had to fight through to the front. On the second lap he was riding as only the stylish Craven could, when suddenly he fell, remounted, and was able to take third place behind How and Jim Lightfoot only after Swede Per Tage Svensson had also gone down.

Samorodov showed what might have been if his hard-charging style had not earned him that earlier exclusion, when he put it over Harrfeldt in the seventh heat. Briggs won the eighth after an argument with McAuliffe on the starting grid, and when Knutsson took second place the final looked wide open.

Greater drama arrived with heat nine when Craven reared at the gate and again on the first turn. He recovered to fill second place behind Boocock, but unexpectedly dropped his bike. The race was stopped and Craven was taken away on a stretcher, knowing that he had just lost his title. The re-run, from which Craven had been excluded anyway, was won by

Samorodov from McAuliffe and Boocock, who had to remount from a fall to claim third place. Briggs won heat 10, but in the next race Knutsson beat Fundin, to place Fundin level with Nordin on eight points after all riders had had three outings. Briggs and Knutsson were on seven, and Samorodov had scored six.

Briggs won the 13th, while Knutsson held back Samorodov in the 14th heat. Fundin beat a dejected Craven in heat 16, and in the 17th Knutsson won to gain a 13-point total for the night. In this race he beat How, who could well have been a contender for major honours if he hadn't already fallen twice. This left Fundin needing to win the 18th heat to claim the title — if he finished second he would have to face a run-off with Knutsson. Fast-gating Peter Moore led for a while, but his effort was short-lived when Fundin got by and took the world championship for the fourth time. Already the Swede was being dubbed the 'greatest rider ever' by his more ardent fans.

Briggs needed to win heat 19 to enforce a run-off with Knutsson for second place overall. But it was not to be — Harrfeldt rode a fine race to keep Briggo at bay, with Nordin third and an obviously pain-racked Craven in last place. Samorodov rounded off a fine night's work by winning heat 20 from Soderman, his spectacular riding arousing the cheers of the crowd.

Barry Briggs leads Ove Fundin during a match race clash. But Fundin won the world title.

1964
Briggs masters the Russians

THE 1964 world final was again staged in Sweden, although this time the venue was the Ullevi track at Gothenburg. Nordic qualifying rounds were raced at Vetlanda, Hammarby and Visby in Sweden, Gislaved in Denmark, and Lahtis in Finland, with the Nordic Final taking place at Odense in Denmark. Continental rounds at Slany in Czechoslovakia, Neubrandenburg in West Germany, Zagreb in Yugoslavia, the Russian Ufa venue and Rybnik in Poland further demonstrated speedway's growing international appeal, and led up to the Continental Final at Slany. The top eight scorers from each of the Nordic and Continental Finals

contested the European Final at Wroclaw in Poland, where home rider Zbigniew Podlecki won from Bjorn Knutsson and Boris Samorodov.

British qualifying rounds were restricted to a preliminary at Rye House, and seven events on National League tracks. With a 15-point maximum Barry Briggs won the British Final at Wembley, from Ken McKinlay and Ron How. The top eight from the British Final met the European top eight at Gothenburg, but one tragically absent name from all these proceedings was that of Peter Craven. The ex-world champion had been killed in a racing accident at the end of 1963; he had ridden in ten consecutive world finals up to that date, and was arguably the most popular rider ever to have contested these events.

A rain-soaked track delayed the start of racing at Gothenburg, and large quantities of sawdust had to be laid before the meeting could get under way. Heat one brought a fine win from the young Russian Gennady Kurilenko, although Cyril Maidment rode aggressively in second place and clashed with Nigel Boocock earlier in the race. An early gathering of potential champions took place in heat two, when reigning world title holder Ove Fundin and European king Podlecki met British No 1 Briggs. Fundin broke into an early lead, to the accompaniment of huge cheers from the partisan crowd, but the celebrations

Feet up and front wheel off the ground, Nigel Boocock keeps ahead of Ken McKinlay.

faded as Briggs rode ahead around the outside of the second bend, to win easily. The accolades were heard again in heat three, when Knutsson had no trouble in beating Mike Broadbanks and McKinlay.

Igor Plechanov demonstrated that the Russian challenge was for real by taking heat four from How, with Samorodov chasing hard in third place after colliding with Pole Andrzej Wyglenda. Heat five saw Fundin beating Knutsson in a clash of the two top Swedes, with Maidment trying to get on terms with them in the fastest race of the night so far. Heat six saw two more big guns line up, Briggs and Plechanov, and after reaching the first turn in the lead the New Zealander held it all the way. By now riding conditions on the track surface had improved.

Samorodov and Kurilenko delivered a Russian 1-2 in heat seven, and heat eight saw the first English win, with How beating Bob Andrews and Podlecki. How was out again in the next race, but Briggs showed him the way home in another rapid time. The giants appeared again in heat 10, but it was really no surprise when the hard-riding Samorodov beat Fundin and McKinlay. Not to be outdone, Plechanov delivered another Russian victory in heat 11, although it was not achieved without incident. Kurilenko fell and forced a re-run, in which a desperate Knutsson crashed on the last bend of the first lap, leaving Plechanov to win from Podlecki, while the Swede remounted to take third place. After Mike Broadbanks's win in heat 12, Briggs was leading the meeting with nine points, Plechanov was only one behind, and Fundin, Samorodov and How had seven.

McKinlay was riding better as the track dried, but he still had to take second place to Plechanov in heat 13. Fundin beat How in heat 15, but the next race virtually settled the destination of the title. A tremendous race between Briggs, Samorodov and Knutsson saw them finish in that order, and although the Russian was beaten he earned a massive cheer from the crowd for his exciting efforts. Samorodov was out again in the next race, but ironically was beaten by Maidment in one of the evening's slower times.

McKinlay, now looking more like the familiar Hurri-Ken of old, was out in heat 19, but was not surprisingly defeated by Briggs, who thus claimed his third world championship. It was the first time since 1959 that a rider had taken the title with an unbeaten score.

Heat 20 was a crucial race for Fundin and Plechanov — if the Russian won he would take the runner-up placing without the need for a run-off, but if the race went to Fundin a decider would be required. Fundin duly led the heat from Plechanov and so after a breather both riders had to line up again. Fundin once more led the way, and the determination of the Russian seemed unable to take him past the track-crafty Swede. But a final full throttle blast on the last bend saw Plechanov get by to win by a disputed half-wheel — not surprisingly, most of the crowd seemed to think that Fundin had kept in front, but not the referee. However, Fundin had the consolation of knowing that his third place meant that he had finished among the top trio in every world final for nine consecutive years — a magnificent achievement by any standards.

Russia's greatest rider, Igor Plechanov (left), on the rostrum with Barry Briggs.

Score Chart

									Total
1 Barry Briggs	New Zealand	3	3	3	3	3			15
2 Igor Plechanov	USSR	3	2	3	3	2			13
3 Ove Fundin	Sweden	2	3	2	3	3			13
4 Boris Samorodov	USSR	1	3	3	2	2			11
5 Bjorn Knutsson	Sweden	3	2	1	1	3			10
Ron How	England	2	3	2	2	1			10
7 Cyril Maidment	England	2	1	1	1	3			8
8 Gennady Kurilenko	USSR	3	2	f/e	1	1			7
9 Mike Broadbanks	England	2	ef	3	ef	1			6
Ken McKinlay	Scotland	1	ef	1	2	2			6
Nigel Boocock	England	0	1	0	3	2			6
12 Andrzej Wyglenda	Poland	0	0	2	2	0			4
Bob Andrews	England	1	2	1	0	0			4
14 Zbigniew Podlecki	Poland	0	1	2	0	0			3
Jaroslav Wolf	Czechoslovakia	0	1	0	1	1			3
16 Dick Fisher	England	1	0	0	ef	0			1
Jim Lightfoot (res)	England	(did not ride)							
Gote Nordin (res)	Sweden	(did not ride)							

NB: Although Andrews was listed in the programme as a New Zealand entrant he was still an English rider but had emigrated.

Heat-by-Heat

		Time
1	Kurilenko, Maidment, Andrews, Boocock	79.5s
2	Briggs, Fundin, Fisher, Podlecki	77.7s
3	Knutsson, Broadbanks, McKinlay, Wolf	79.3s
4	Plechanov, How, Samorodov, Wyglenda	76.7s
5	Fundin, Knutsson, Maidment, Wyglenda	76.3s
6	Briggs, Plechanov, Boocock, Broadbanks (ef)	76.6s
7	Samorodov, Kurilenko, Wolf, Fisher	77.6s
8	How, Andrews, Podlecki, McKinlay (ef)	79.3s
9	Briggs, How, Maidment, Wolf	76.7s
10	Samorodov, Fundin, McKinlay, Boocock	76.2s
11	Plechanov, Podlecki, Knutsson (f/re), Kurilenko (f/exc)	76.2s
12	Broadbanks, Wyglenda, Andrews, Fisher	79.1s
13	Plechanov, McKinlay, Maidment, Fisher (ef)	76.0s
14	Boocock, Wyglenda, Wolf, Podlecki	78.9s
15	Fundin, How, Kurilenko, Broadbanks (ef)	77.4s
16	Briggs, Samorodov, Knutsson, Andrews	78.6s
17	Maidment, Samorodov, Broadbanks, Podlecki	79.0s
18	Knutsson, Boocock, How, Fisher	78.1s
19	Briggs, McKinlay, Kurilenko, Wyglenda	78.1s
20	Fundin, Plechanov, Wolf, Andrews	77.6s
21	Plechanov beat Fundin in run-off for 2nd place	76.8s

1965
Knutsson's finest hour

AFTER A SEASON'S absence, the world final returned to Wembley stadium in 1965, much to the delight of the British crowds. By this time the former Provincial and National Leagues had amalgamated into a new arrangement known simply as the British League. To cater for the few tracks remaining outside this organisation, British qualifying rounds began in May with events on five of the non-league circuits. Each of the 18 British League tracks then ran an eliminator, the top 32 scorers contesting the semi-finals at Poole and Glasgow White City. The top eight from each semi moved on to the British Final at West Ham in August, where Barry Briggs won from Nigel Boocock and Ken McKinlay. This trio and the next five highest scorers qualified for Wembley.

Nordic rounds took place at Vetlanda, Boras, and Visby in Sweden, Norway's Skien circuit and the Danish Frederika track, with the Nordic final returning to Skien. Meanwhile Continental qualifiers were being staged at Graz in Austria, Miskolc in Hungary, Abensburg and Neubrandenburg in West Germany, Lvov in Russia and Ljubljana in Yugoslavia, while Poland ran the Continental Final at Wroclaw. Ove Fundin won the European Final at Slany in Czechoslovakia, leading a run-off with Bjorn Knutsson after each had scored 14 points. As usual, the next six highest scorers joined the leading pair at Wembley.

Shock results were the order of the day from the start, when an on-form Boocock beat Fundin in the opening heat, with Leif Larsson and Lubos Tomicek third and fourth. Then England's Brian Brett won heat two from Andrzej Pogorzelski, Jimmy Gooch and McKinlay, and Bengt Jansson completed a hat-trick of upsets in the next heat, leading home Knutsson from Antoni Woryna and Reg Luckhurst. Still another surprise came in heat four when Igor Plechanov beat Briggs, Soren Sjosten and Andrzej Wyglenda. These freak results meant that after each rider had raced once, no obvious favourite for the title had emerged.

The real eliminating process started in heats five and six, with Briggs winning the fifth as Brett trailed in last, and Sjosten took the next from Pogorzelski, with previous heat winners Jansson and Boocock filling the minor roles. By winning the seventh heat Plechanov shaped up as the rider most likely to succeed, while in the eighth the rivalry between Fundin and Knutsson

was again put to the test: Knutsson won, forcing his opponent to drop a point.

Knutsson won again in the 10th, and a crucial victory it turned out to be. His victim this time was Plechanov, who thus dropped his first point of the night. In third and fourth places, Brett and Boocock could now be certain that they had blown their chances. Sjosten took the 11th heat, while the evergreen Fundin beat Jansson in the 12th. Briggs was third and McKinlay last in this tight struggle of top men.

Sjosten's chances took a dive in heat 13 when he was beaten by Knutsson, and Briggs hit back with a victory over Boocock in the next race. Brett also revived his form to win heat 15 impressively from Jansson and Wyglenda, while Larsson fell. Heat 16 brought a renewal of the previous year's tussle between Fundin and Plechanov: the Swede won, but was made to work hard.

Plechanov was out again in the 17th heat, and made no mistake against Jansson to finish his night's work with a 13-point score. Russia's chances of winning the World Speedway Championship for the first time now depended, ironically, on whether Sweden's Knutsson could beat Briggs in the 19th heat. However, before that the crowd were treated to a classic battle of tactics

Score Chart

								Total
1	Bjorn Knutsson	Sweden	2	3	3	3	3	14
2	Igor Plechanov	USSR	3	3	2	2	3	13
3	Ove Fundin	Sweden	2	2	3	3	3	13
4	Barry Briggs	New Zealand	2	3	1	3	1	10
	Bengt Jansson	Sweden	3	1	2	2	2	10
6	Brian Brett	England	3	0	1	3	2	9
	Soren Sjosten	Sweden	1	3	3	2	0	9
8	Nigel Boocock	England	3	0	0	2	3	8
9	Andrzej Pogorzelski	Poland	2	2	3	0	f/r	7
10	Antoni Woryna	Poland	1	2	2	0	1	6
11	Leif Larsson	Sweden	1	0	2	f	2	5
	Reg Luckhurst	England	0	2	1	1	1	5
13	Ken McKinlay	Scotland	0	1	0	1	2	4
14	Jimmy Gooch	England	1	1	0	1	0	3
15	Lubos Tomicek	Czechoslovakia	0	1	0	0	1	2
	Andrzej Wyglenda	Poland	0	0	1	1	0	2
	Mike Broadbanks (res)	England	(did not ride)					
	Marian Rose (res)	Poland	(did not ride)					

Heat-by-Heat

		Time
1	Boocock, Fundin, Larsson, Tomicek	69.6s
2	Brett, Pogorzelski, Gooch, McKinlay	69.6s
3	Jansson, Knutsson, Woryna, Luckhurst	69.0s
4	Plechanov, Briggs, Sjosten, Wyglenda	69.0s
5	Briggs, Luckhurst, Tomicek, Brett	70.0s
6	Sjosten, Pogorzelski, Jansson, Boocock	70.2s
7	Plechanov, Woryna, McKinlay, Larsson	69.2s
8	Knutsson, Fundin, Gooch, Wyglenda	69.4s
9	Pogorzelski, Woryna, Wyglenda, Tomicek	70.8s
10	Knutsson, Plechanov, Brett, Boocock	69.6s
11	Sjosten, Larsson, Luckhurst, Gooch	70.2s
12	Fundin, Jansson, Briggs, McKinlay	69.4s
13	Knutsson, Sjosten, McKinlay, Tomicek	70.2s
14	Briggs, Boocock, Gooch, Woryna	70.4s
15	Brett, Jansson, Wyglenda, Larsson (f)	70.8s
16	Fundin, Plechanov, Luckhurst, Pogorzelski	69.0s
17	Plechanov, Jansson, Tomicek, Gooch	69.2s
18	Boocock, McKinlay, Luckhurst, Wyglenda	70.6s
19	Knutsson, Larsson, Briggs, Pogorzelski (f/re)	70.8s
20	Fundin, Brett, Woryna, Sjosten	70.8s
21	Plechanov beat Fundin in run-off for 2nd place	69.8s

between Boocock and McKinlay in heat 18, the former reaching the flag first.

In the deciding 19th heat, Knutsson rapidly crushed Russian aspirations by leading all the way and claiming what was to be his only world championship, after twice finishing as runner-up. Larsson beat Briggs into third place in this penultimate race.

Fundin needed a win in heat 20 to force a run-off for second and third overall placings. He duly beat Brett, but in the run-off the man he had to meet was none other than Plechanov, who had beaten the Swede in a deciding race for second place overall only the previous year. And not only were the riders the same, but the result was identical, with Plechanov taking a deserved victory and holding on to his world No 2 honours for the second successive year. Fundin's reward was the knowledge that he had now reached the top three in world finals for an incredible ten consecutive years.

At this point in his career, the top Englishman in 1965, Brian Brett, looked as though he might fill the gap in British speedway left by the death of Peter Craven. His nine points at Wembley were well earned and placed him sixth overall in his first world final. However, he was to retire prematurely and never realised his full potential as a dirt track exponent.

1966
A world final in one race

WITH EASTERN EUROPEAN countries having been so forcefully represented in recent world finals, it was hardly surprising that the Polish and Russian speedway authorities should press for better representation in the running of qualifying rounds. Thus, although the 1966 final was again allocated to Sweden, qualifying procedures for British riders became even tougher. After the preliminary eliminators they had to contest semi-finals, a British Final, then a Nordic-British Final and eventually a European Final at Wembley. This meant that Britons who seriously intended to win through to Gothenburg would first have to endure no less than seven qualifying meetings.

For the record, the British semi-finals took place at Cradley Heath and Halifax, with the British Final going to Wimbledon and the Nordic-British event being staged at Sheffield. Continental rounds were held throughout Eastern Europe, with the leading scorers moving on to a Continental Final at the Slany oval in Czechoslovakia, the top eight men then meeting the best of the Nordic-British contestants at Wembley, from which the 10 most successful riders reached the World Final. Swedish tracks had held their own qualifiers, and fed their six best riders to Gothenburg.

For the first time in 13 years Ove Fundin did not contest the world final. His absence — he had been suspended prior to the qualifiers and was unable to compete — seemed to leave a gap in the atmosphere, and Swedish hopes sank further when Bengt Jansson broke an ankle during the qualifying rounds and was unable to appear at Gothenburg.

Even more stunning for the 34,000 crowd was the retirement of reigning champion Bjorn Knutsson from the first heat when his engine dropped a valve. This left Pole Antoni Woryna to win. There were understandable cheers for Swede Gote Nordin when he won heat two, even though he was riding on makeshift equipment after his best machines had been stolen. Norwegian Sverre Harrfeldt was a popular winner of the third heat from Ivan Mauger, while Barry Briggs showed his liking for Gothenburg's Ullevi bowl by taking heat four from Leif Enecrona and a disappointing Igor Plechanov. Plechanov was beaten again in the next race, this time by Woryna, but at least this time the Russian rode with more spirit to keep Mauger back in third place. Pole Stanislaw Tkocz won

In the European final at Wembley, Antoni Woryna leads, from left, Barry Briggs, Marian Kaiser and George Hunter.

the sixth heat and Harrfeldt took the seventh from a fighting Nordin. Knutsson trailed in third, knowing that his title had already disappeared.

Heats eight and nine were crucial for Briggs, who was riding in intense pain from a damaged shoulder. In the eighth Torbjorn Harrysson gated ahead of Briggs, but led him for only a short while until the New Zealander got past. Harrysson was left to gamely snap at the heels of the leader. As it happened, heat nine was to encapsulate this entire world final in one race. Harrfeldt hit the first turn in the lead, but one lap later Briggs slipped inside and opened up an unbeatable lead. Woryna was third, and these were the only points that the Pole and Harrfeldt were to drop. The end result of the final only repeated the placings in this crucial heat.

Mauger came into his own in heat 11, beating Enecrona and Knutsson with a display of cool temperament that exactly matched the big occasion. Nordin and Harrysson had a battle royal in front of

Plechanov in the 12th heat, even though Harrysson had missed the gate. Woryna, Harrfeldt and Briggs won the next three races without trouble, and Mauger took his second victory of the night in heat 16, although Harrysson fought back from another bad start and became the hero of the home fans.

Woryna won the 17th heat, and with a total score of 13 points had ensured himself a place among the top three. But the fate of the championship itself was sealed in the next race when Briggs beat Mauger, to emerge with a maximum score just as he had confirmed his 1964 title. It was Briggs's fourth world championship, equalling Fundin's record. The victory had not been as easy as his points tally suggested, however, for in addition to coping with his injured shoulder his bike had suffered carburettor trouble after his win in heat nine, and some frantic welding was necessary to repair the machine in time for his next outing in heat 15. Briggs, incidentally, was the first rider to win the world title on the Czech Jawa-ESO machine, which was later to be known simply as the Jawa. Plechanov's two runner-up positions in earlier finals had also been achieved on these bikes, which in future years were to largely replace the British JAP as the premier speedway machine.

Briggs loaned his Jawa-ESO to Knutsson for the 19th heat, and the Swede promptly won the race from Plechanov. The last race was to decide the overall runner-up position, Harrfeldt winning the race from the aggressive Harrysson. Harrfeldt had also had his share of problems, having to race after recently recovering from an internal operation. Woryna, however, was proud enough with his third overall placing, as he was the first Pole ever to reach the top three in a world final. But the question that all the Swedish fans were asking was, what would have happened if the great Fundin had raced at Gothenburg?

Score Chart

								Total
1	Barry Briggs	New Zealand	3	3	3	3	3	15
2	Sverre Harrfeldt	Norway	3	3	2	3	3	14
3	Antoni Woryna	Poland	3	3	1	3	3	13
4	Ivan Mauger	New Zealand	2	1	3	3	2	11
5	Torbjorn Harrysson	Sweden	2	2	2	2	2	10
6	Gote Nordin	Sweden	3	2	3	f	1	9
7	Leif Enecrona	Sweden	2	1	2	2	1	8
	Igor Plechanov	USSR	1	2	1	2	2	8
9	Stanislaw Tkocz	Poland	1	3	2	1	0	7
10	Bjorn Knutsson	Sweden	ef	1	1	ef	3	5
	Marian Kaiser	Poland	0	0	3	1	1	5
	Andrzej Pogorzelski	Poland	2	2	0	1	ef	5
13	Mike Broadbanks	England	1	1	0	0	2	4
14	Leif Larsson	Sweden	1	0	0	0	3	3
15	Nigel Boocock	England	0	0	1	0	1	2
16	Peo Soderman	Sweden	0	exc	0	1	0	1
	Bengt Brannefors (res)	Sweden	(did not ride)					
	Ken McKinlay (res)	Scotland	(did not ride)					

Heat-by-Heat

		Time
1	Woryna, Harrysson, Tkocz, Knutsson (ef)	78.0s
2	Nordin, Pogorzelski, Broadbanks, Soderman	79.1s
3	Harrfeldt, Mauger, Larsson, Kaiser	78.2s
4	Briggs, Enecrona, Plechanov, Boocock	77.5s
5	Woryna, Plechanov, Mauger, Soderman (exc)	77.6s
6	Tkocz, Pogorzelski, Enecrona, Larsson	78.4s
7	Harrfeldt, Nordin, Knutsson, Boocock	78.5s
8	Briggs, Harrysson, Broadbanks, Kaiser	78.7s
9	Briggs, Harrfeldt, Woryna, Pogorzelski	78.4s
10	Kaiser, Tkocz, Boocock, Soderman	79.0s
11	Mauger, Enecrona, Knutsson, Broadbanks	78.4s
12	Nordin, Harrysson, Plechanov, Larsson	78.0s
13	Woryna, Enecrona, Kaiser, Nordin (f)	78.1s
14	Harrfeldt, Plechanov, Tkocz, Broadbanks	78.7s
15	Briggs, Larsson, Soderman, Knutsson (ef)	78.2s
16	Mauger, Harrysson, Pogorzelski, Boocock	78.9s
17	Woryna, Broadbanks, Boocock, Larsson	80.0s
18	Briggs, Mauger, Nordin, Tkocz	78.0s
19	Knutsson, Plechanov, Kaiser, Pogorzelski (ef)	79.3s
20	Harrfeldt, Harrysson, Enecrona, Soderman	79.0s

Gote Nordin, who scored nine points in Sweden, crinkles the rear tyre of his Jawa.

1967
The master coaches the pupil

Russian Igor Plechanov confers with Poland's Antoni Woryna (right) in the pits.

Score Chart

								Total
1 Ove Fundin	Sweden	3	3	3	2	3	14	
2 Bengt Jansson	Sweden	2	3	3	3	3	14	
3 Ivan Mauger	New Zealand	3	3	3	2	2	13	
4 Igor Plechanov	USSR	2	3	3	3	1	12	
5 Barry Briggs	New Zealand	1	2	2	3	3	11	
6 Eric Boocock	England	3	2	1	1	2	9	
Anders Michanek	Sweden	0	2	2	3	2	9	
8 Ray Wilson	England	3	f	1	1	2	7	
9 Bernt Persson	Sweden	2	1	1	2	f/e	6	
Andrzej Pogorzelski	Poland	2	2	0	1	1	6	
11 Antoni Woryna	Poland	1	1	2	1	0	5	
Rick France	England	1	1	0	2	1	5	
13 Colin Pratt	England	0	0	1	0	3	4	
14 Jerzy Trzeskowski	Poland	f	0	2	0	1	3	
15 Andrzej Wyglenda	Poland	1	1	0	0	0	2	
16 Jochen Dinse	E Germany	f/r	0	0	0	0	0	
Mike Broadbanks (res)	England	(did not ride)						
Leif Enecrona (res)	Sweden	(did not ride)						

Heat-by-heat

		Time
1	Wilson, Persson, Wyglenda, Dinse (f/re)	72.0s
2	Fundin, Jansson, Briggs, Michanek	70.6s
3	Boocock, Pogorzelski, Woryna, Pratt	69.8s
4	Mauger, Plechanov, France, Trzeskowski (f)	71.2s
5	Jansson, Pogorzelski, Wyglenda, Trzeskowski	69.8s
6	Plechanov, Briggs, Persson, Pratt	69.6s
7	Fundin, Boocock, France, Wilson (f)	70.6s
8	Mauger, Michanek, Woryna, Dinse	71.4s
9	Mauger, Briggs, Boocock, Wyglenda	71.2s
10	Jansson, Woryna, Persson, France	71.6s
11	Plechanov, Michanek, Wilson, Pogorzelski	69.8s
12	Fundin, Trzeskowski, Pratt, Dinse	72.8s
13	Plechanov, Fundin, Woryna, Wyglenda	69.4s
14	Michanek, Persson, Boocock, Trzeskowski	70.4s
15	Jansson, Mauger, Wilson, Pratt	70.6s
16	Briggs, France, Pogorzelski, Dinse	71.0s
17	Pratt, Michanek, France, Wyglenda	71.4s
18	Fundin, Mauger, Pogorzelski, Persson (f/exc)	72.0s
19	Briggs, Wilson, Trzeskowski, Woryna	71.2s
20	Jansson, Boocock, Plechanov, Dinse	70.4s
21	Fundin beat Jansson in run-off for 1st place	71.4s

THE SEE-SAW between Britain and Sweden as host nations for the world final continued in 1967, with the event returning to the Empire Stadium at Wembley once again. British qualifying rounds were staged on the league tracks, now numbering 19, and the top 32 scorers went into the semi-finals at Sheffield and Wimbledon. Barry Briggs won the British Final at West Ham from Ivan Mauger, with Eric Boocock, qualifying for his first world final, in third place.

Nordic qualifying rounds were raced at Visby, Malilla, and Vetlanda in Sweden and at Hillerod in Denmark, with the final being held at Selskov in Norway. Continental rounds were spread as far afield as Maribor in Yugoslavia, Misnia in East Germany, Abensberg in West Germany, and Miskolc in Hungary, with semi-finals taking place at Balakowie in Russia and Czechoslovakia's popular Slany track. From the Continental Final at Kempten in West Germany, the top eight scorers joined the top eight from the Nordic Final in the European Final at Wroclaw in Poland. The top ten from this event joined the top six Britons at Wembley.

Heat one brought a delightful spectacle for the home fans — England's Ray Wilson winning his first ever race in a world final, from Swede Bernt Persson. After his absence the previous season, Ove Fundin made a storming return to world championship competition by winning heat two in a much faster time, from a high class field consisting of Bengt Jansson, Briggs and Anders Michanek, who finished in that order. Eric Boocock also won his world final debut race in an even faster time than the opening heats, but Mauger made hard work of beating Igor Plechanov in heat four.

Jansson gave a hint of things to come by winning heat five from three Poles, while Plechanov showed his true class by leading home Briggs and Persson in the next heat. Fundin claimed the seventh heat from Boocock and Rick France after the impetuous Wilson had fallen. Mauger had to ride in heats eight and nine, but won them both, beating Michanek and Antoni Woryna in the first and Briggs and Boocock in the next.

Ove Fundin leads Bengt Jansson in the crucial run-off for the title.

With three victories from three rides, Mauger was looking strong at this stage.

Jansson confirmed that his earlier heat win was no fluke by taking heat 10 from Woryna and Persson, and Plechanov, riding at his storming best, beat Michanek and Wilson in heat 11. But Fundin took the 12th race to equal Mauger's unbeaten feat after all riders had had three outings. Jansson and Plechanov had dropped only a single point each.

Heat 13 was unlucky for Fundin — he was soundly thrashed by Plechanov, who recorded the fastest time of the night in the process. Woryna trailed in third, and was never in contention after that. Michanek won the 14th heat from Persson, and when the crucial 15th brought Jansson and Mauger together, the Swede won, while Mauger delegated third place to Wilson. After Briggs had won heat 16, all riders had had four outings and an incredibly tense finale was shaping up, for there were no less than four men sharing the lead at that stage. Fundin, Jansson, Mauger and Plechanov each had 11 points, and to raise the tension even higher, the crowd knew that decisive races between Fundin and Mauger, and then Jansson and Plechanov, were still to come in the remaining four heats.

Colin Pratt won heat 17 from a surprised Michanek, but the first of the big duels came next. Fundin, Mauger and Persson lined up, but the race had to be restarted when the latter fell and was excluded. The outcome of the re-run was a win for Fundin, which crushed Mauger's chances of taking overall victory. Briggs won the 19th heat from Wilson, but everyone was waiting for the crucial last race in which Jansson and Plechanov were to meet. If Plechanov won he would earn the right to a run-off for the title with his great adversary, Fundin. If Jansson won he would face up to Fundin in a run-off, but if Boocock or even the unfancied East German Jochen Dinse took the last race, Fundin would inherit the title unchallenged.

Matters were settled when the fast-gating Jansson broke into an early lead, and Plechanov was unable to get past the stylish Boocock. The re-run itself evolved into an anti-climax, as Fundin was sharper at the gate and never looked in trouble as he beat Jansson by 50 yards: it was a case of the old master giving a sharp lesson to the young pupil.

So Fundin took the world championship for a record fifth occasion, but surprisingly he had never scored a maximum in reaching any of his victories. Jansson was a worthy runner-up, while Mauger had climbed to third place in only his second world final. But it would have been a brave prophet at that stage who would have suggested that a decade later Mauger would have a record of world championship wins to equal Fundin's.

1968

The emergence of Mauger the unbeatable

WHEN THE world final returned to Gothenburg in 1968, there were many forecasts that Barry Briggs would win the title again on his favoured Ullevi track. But reigning champion Ove Fundin was also expected to perform well in front of his home fans in the hopes of gaining a sixth championship, while Anders Michanek had matured into a real force, and Ivan Mauger had been in great form this season and was also a threat.

A crowd of almost 47,000 watched what turned out to be one of the dullest world finals ever, and veteran speedway observers were left wondering whether modern day professionalism was replacing the traditional hectic action with a more clinical brand of racing.

Heat one saw Michanek take a popular victory over England's Martin Ashby, the two Polish contestants both falling at different stages of the race. In heat two Mauger showed that he was in Sweden for no other purpose than to win races, leaving Briggs at the gate

The dynamic style of Torbjorn Harrysson enlivened the 1968 final as he battled to a 10-point total.

and never being headed. Pole Edward Jancarz and Norway's Reidar Eide were never in contention.

Gennady Kurilenko was fast away in heat three, but Torbjorn Harrysson, emulating the dynamic style of the late Peter Craven, rode round the Russian on the first turn to take a winning lead. Swedes Hasse Holmqvist and Gunnar Malmqvist were left at the back to make no impression on the leaders. Fundin earned massive cheers from the crowd in an exciting heat four. He gated well, but Bernt Persson blased round all three of his rivals, only to suffer engine failure when leading. Meanwhile Antoni Woryna had moved past Fundin, but the track-crafty Swede repassed on the last lap to win his first outing of the night. After everyone had ridden once it was clear that track conditions favoured the fastest gaters, while Mauger and Fundin were shaping as potential winners, and the unhappy Briggs was suffering from a high temperature caused by a virus infection.

Score Chart

							Total
1 Ivan Mauger	New Zealand	3	3	3	3	3	15
2 Barry Briggs	New Zealand	2	2	3	3	2	12
3 Edward Jancarz	Poland	1	3	1	3	3	11
4 Gennady Kurilenko	USSR	2	3	3	1	2	11
5 Torbjorn Harrysson	Sweden	3	3	2	1	1	10
Pawel Waloszek	Poland	f	2	3	2	3	10
7 Anders Michanek	Sweden	3	1	2	2	1	9
Hasse Holmqvist	Sweden	1	2	2	2	2	9
9 Ove Fundin	Sweden	3	0	1	0	3	7
Gunnar Malmqvist	Sweden	0	2	1	3	1	7
11 Antoni Woryna	Poland	2	1	ret	1	1	5
Martin Ashby	England	2	1	0	2	0	5
13 Reidar Eide	Norway	0	0	2	1	f	3
Jerzy Trzeszkowski	Poland	f	1	0	0	2	3
15 Bernt Persson	Sweden	ef	0	1	0	0	1
Nigel Boocock	England	1	0	0	f/e	ef	1
Igor Plechanov (res)	USSR	(did not ride)					
Jerzy Padewski (res)	Poland	(did not ride)					

Heat-by-heat

		Time
1	Michanek, Ashby, Waloszek (f), Trzeszkowski (f)	77.4s
2	Mauger, Briggs, Jancarz, Eide	77.0s
3	Harrysson, Kurilenko, Holmqvist, Malmqvist	78.5s
4	Fundin, Woryna, Boocock, Persson (ef)	79.3s
5	Kurilenko, Briggs, Michanek, Boocock	79.0s
6	Mauger, Holmqvist, Ashby, Persson	79.0s
7	Jancarz, Malmqvist, Trzeszkowski, Fundin	78.0s
8	Harrysson, Waloszek, Woryna, Eide	78.8s
9	Mauger, Michanek, Malmqvist, Woryna (ret)	79.0s
10	Briggs, Harrysson, Fundin, Ashby	79.0s
11	Kurilenko, Eide, Persson, Trzeszkowski	78.5s
12	Waloszek, Holmqvist, Jancarz, Boocock	78.0s
13	Jancarz, Michanek, Harrysson, Persson	77.7s
14	Malmqvist, Ashby, Eide, Boocock (f/exc)	78.5s
15	Briggs, Holmqvist, Woryna, Trzeszkowski	78.0s
16	Mauger, Waloszek, Kurilenko, Fundin	79.0s
17	Fundin, Holmqvist, Michanek, Eide (f)	79.5s
18	Jancarz, Kurilenko, Woryna, Ashby	77.2s
19	Mauger, Trzeszkowski, Harrysson (f/re), Boocock (ef)	78.0s
20	Waloszek, Briggs, Malmqvist, Persson	79.0s
21	Jancarz beat Kurilenko for 3rd place.	no time

Kurilenko led Briggs all the way in heat five, with Michanek in third spot ahead of Nigel Boocock. Mauger settled heat six promptly with a lightning start, the only change in places occurring when Ashby passed Persson into third place, with Holmqvist holding onto second berth. Heat seven was another processional race, although it was traumatic for Fundin when he was crowded on the first turn and was never able to pull up from last place. The defeat spelled the end of Fundin's title hopes, while Jancarz was the race winner.

Heat eight saw a repetition of events in heat three, when Harrysson again rode round the field to the delight of the Swedish supporters. Pawel Waloszek's good challenge was to no avail. Mauger was again in superb gating form in the next race, Michanek's early challenge fading before the first lap was over. For once Harrysson hit the first turn in the lead in heat 10, but he needed to with Fundin and Briggs forming his opposition. Despite his ailment Briggs fought past Fundin and gave chase to Harrysson, passing him and just hanging on for victory in a great race.

Heat 11 saw Kurilenko break the tapes at the start, but he made no mistake in the re-run and led all the way from Eide and Persson, with Pole Jerzy Trzeszkowski a long way behind. After Waloszek had won heat 12 all riders had had three outings, leaving Mauger unbeaten in the lead, Kurilenko and Harrysson only one point behind, and Briggs having dropped two.

The pressure seemed to tell on Harrysson in the 13th heat. Jancarz broke the tapes, but in the re-run he pulled his concentration together to burst into the lead and shrug off the challenge from the young Swede. Then Michanek got past Harrysson, and the latter's title hopes slumped when he only just managed to hang on to third place in front of Persson.

Nigel Boocock was hurt in a first bend pile-up in heat 14, and his feelings also suffered damage when he was excluded from the re-run for being the primary cause of the crash. The restarted race was a bore, with Malmqvist leading all the way from Ashby. Briggs showed that he was winning the battle with his virus by taking heat 15.

Heat 16 was to be the decisive race, featuring Mauger, Kurilenko, Fundin and Waloszek. Mauger led from the gate again, and Waloszek helped the Kiwi's cause by keeping Kurilenko in third place. It was a sad sight when Fundin finished almost half a lap behind in this race, but in the next heat he reversed his form by putting in a great ride to beat Holmqvist, Michanek and Eide. Jancarz earned himself a run-off for third place with Kurilenko by beating the Russian in heat 18, but in the next race Mauger needed only a third place to lift the world championship. There was never any doubt about the outcome — he again streamed from the gate first to win from Trzeszkowski and take his first title.

Briggs was visibly tiring in the final heat when he was beaten by Waloszek, but his 12-point score was still good enough to give him second place overall. In the run-off for third place Jancarz rode a great race from the gate to beat the determined Kurilenko.

1969 Mauger untroubled again

BY 1969 the world speedway authorities had still not allocated a final to the emergent Eastern European countries, and so the event reverted to Wembley once again. A top class field attracted 75,000 spectators for the big night, many of them wondering whether Ove Fundin, the speedway legend, could take his sixth title. His renowned ability on the tight Wembley curves was a contributing factor to this speculation.

The meeting started with a runaway win for Nigel Boocock in the first heat, with Torbjorn Harrysson second and Poles Jan Mucha and Andrzej Wyglenda never in the hunt. Heat two turned into a difficult test for Fundin: Edward Jancarz and Soren Sjosten broke the tapes, and in the restart Sjosten led from Henryk Glucklich, with Jancarz and Fundin in the rear. There was plenty of pushing and shoving in the first turn, and when Glucklich drifted wide on the next bend Fundin

and Jancarz broke free of the melee to finish second and third behind the flying Sjosten.

Heat three saw reigning champion Ivan Mauger and Russian Valeri Klementiev leading from the gate, but the latter almost eliminated himself from the meeting when he left things late at the first turn. Meanwhile Mauger skated away to win followed by Hasse Holmqvist, and Howard Cole, who was riding in what was to be his only world final, filled third place.

Heat four drew big gasps from the crowd as Ken McKinlay streaked away from Ronnie Moore, Barry Briggs and Andrzej Pogorzelski. Riding like a man possessed, McKinlay held on to his lead until the final lap, when he drifted wide and Moore and Briggs grabbed the opportunity to ride through the gap. Then Moore also slid out, and Briggs moved up to win a fantastic race that he surely must have thought he was going to lose.

McKinlay was out again in heat five, but this time he made no mistake to win comfortably from Harrysson and Holmqvist. Sjosten fell on the second lap, a disaster that was to appear even more costly as the meeting progressed. Pogorzelski led from the tapes in heat six, but Boocock and Jancarz provided good racing for second and third places, finishing in that order.

Becoming even more notorious for his lightning starts, Mauger pulled another fast one over Fundin in heat seven, and from that point on the outcome of the race was never in doubt. Moore finished third, clearly in pain from an injured right foot. Klementiev drew the cheers of the crowd in heat eight, easily leading Briggs

Magnificent Wembley action as Soren Sjosten holds the inside line from Edward Jancarz.

all the way with a spectacular display of spirit. Wyglenda and Glucklich were third and fourth.

The ninth heat brought disaster for the plucky Swede, Harrysson. Mauger and Jancarz got out in front, but they seemed to touch and when the Pole got his bike crossed up sideways Harrysson ploughed into him, breaking a leg in the accident. A saddened crowd hardly raised a ripple in the re-run, when Mauger beat Briggs in the fastest time of the night so far.

Heat 10 degenerated into a real mix-up, first when a restart was ordered, and then when Klementiev and Boocock tangled. The Russian was excluded from the second re-run, which Boocock won from Sjosten and Moore. Holmqvist won the next race after chasing Mucha for three laps, while heat 12 saw an old-timers' battle take place between McKinlay and Fundin. McKinlay saw off the Swede's challenge, and after all riders had completed three races Mauger remained unbeaten, Boocock had dropped only one point, and Briggs and McKinlay were two down on seven points each.

Klementiev ran into serious trouble in heat 13, first breaking the tapes and then falling in the re-run while chasing the field. Fundin won from Pogorzelski and Zbigniew Podlecki, who had replaced the injured Harrysson. Mauger was beaten out of the gate for the first time in heat 14, but Glucklich's fortunes were short-lived when the Kiwi emerged from the first turn in first place. Boocock and McKinlay finished third and fourth, equally unable to come to terms with Mauger's flying pace. Sjosten made the gate in front of Briggs and Mucha in heat 15, and a shock hit the crowd as Briggs over-cooked it in one of the turns and Mucha grabbed second place. Jancarz displayed real class by passing Moore and Holmqvist from the back in heat 16, and at that stage, with each man having completed four rides, Mauger was out on his own in front, certain to finish among the top two even if he did not contest his last heat.

Heat 17 produced some good racing among the also-rans, with Glucklich winning. All four of the contenders in heat 18 were vying for runner-up position overall, and Briggs won in the fastest time of the night followed by Holmqvist and Boocock, with Fundin in a sorry last place.

McKinlay must almost have used psychic powers in the 19th heat, when he missed the gate and kept out of trouble as Jancarz, Mucha and Klementiev chopped, changed, barged and bumped each other for the whole race. It was dangerous stuff, and Jancarz rightly drew the applause of the crowd when he won from Mucha.

Briggs and Sjosten had amassed only 11 points each after their five rides, so Mauger was already the world champion for the second year before he even started in heat 20. And maybe he thought he was back at Belle Vue when he seemed to team-ride with his partner at the Manchester track, Sjosten, allowing the Swede to win and gain a run-off with Briggs for second place overall. Mauger was loudly booed by the crowd, but he could afford to shrug off some temporary unpopularity.

After Briggs had made a prolonged and detailed inspection of the starting area, he won the run-off and second place in the championship, while Sjosten waited patiently in the race for the mistake that never came.

Score Chart

								Total
1 Ivan Mauger	New Zealand	3	3	3	3	2	14
2 Barry Briggs	New Zealand	3	2	2	1	3	11
3 Soren Sjosten	Sweden	3	f	2	3	3	11
4 Nigel Boocock	England	3	2	3	1	1	10
Hasse Holmqvist	Sweden	2	1	3	2	2	10
6 Edward Jancarz	Poland	1	1	1	3	3	9
Ove Fundin	Sweden	2	2	2	3	0	9
8 Ken McKinlay	Scotland	1	3	3	0	0	7
Andrzej Pogorzelski	Poland	0	3	1	2	1	7
Jan Mucha	Poland	1	0	2	2	2	7
11 Ronnie Moore	New Zealand	2	1	1	1	1	6
12 Henryk Glucklich	Poland	0	0	0	2	3	5
13 Valeri Klementiev	USSR	0	3	f	f	1	4
Torbjorn Harrysson	Sweden	2	2	f	ns	ns	4
15 Andrzej Wyglenda	Poland	0	1	1	0	0	2
16 Howard Cole	England	1	0	0	0	0	1
Zbigniew Podlecki (res)	Poland				1	2	3
Arnold Haley (res)	England	(did not ride)					

Heat-by-heat

		Time
1	Boocock, Harrysson, Mucha, Wyglenda	71.2s
2	Sjosten, Fundin, Jancarz, Glucklich	71.8s
3	Mauger, Holmqvist, Cole, Klementiev	71.4s
4	Briggs, Moore, McKinlay, Pogorzelski	71.8s
5	McKinlay, Harrysson, Holmqvist, Sjosten (f)	71.4s
6	Pogorzelski, Boocock, Jancarz, Cole	70.6s
7	Mauger, Fundin, Moore, Mucha	70.8s
8	Klementiev, Briggs, Wyglenda, Glucklich	71.0s
9	Mauger, Briggs, Jancarz, Harrysson (f/exc)	70.2s
10	Boocock, Sjosten, Moore, Klementiev (f/exc)	71.4s
11	Holmqvist, Mucha, Pogorzelski, Glucklich	70.8s
12	McKinlay, Fundin, Wyglenda, Cole	72.2s
13	Fundin, Pogorzelski, Podlecki, Klementiev (f)	71.0s
14	Mauger, Glucklich, Boocock, McKinlay	70.4s
15	Sjosten, Mucha, Briggs, Cole	70.6s
16	Jancarz, Holmqvist, Moore, Wyglenda	70.8s
17	Glucklich, Podlecki, Moore, Cole	70.6s
18	Briggs, Holmqvist, Boocock, Fundin	70.2s
19	Jancarz, Mucha, Klementiev, McKinlay	71.0s
20	Sjosten, Mauger, Pogorzelski, Wyglenda	71.4s
	Briggs beat Sjosten in run-off for 2nd place	70.2s

Consistent Ken McKinlay leads Barry Briggs.

The World Championship 1970-78

Just as the sixties saw world finals staged in Scandinavia for the first time, so the seventies provided a new host country, Poland. The decade was also notable for the appearance of Eastern Europe's first world champion, Ivan Mauger's record-equalling fifth championship, and the searing performances of Denmark's Ole Olsen.

Ole Olsen, the man who stamped his authority on world championship speedway in the seventies, pictured in full flight in the 1977 Inter-Continental final leading Australia's John Boulger.

1970
Full of Eastern challenge

WITH THE ARRIVAL of the seventies came the first occasion that the world final was staged in Eastern Europe. Riders from Iron Curtain countries had improved so much in recent years that it was obvious that claims for an Eastern-based final could not be delayed for much longer. But perhaps the speedway authorities could have timed better their removal of the event to Wroclaw's Olympic Stadium in Poland, as 1970 represented the 25th running of the World Speedway Championship, and in this Silver Jubilee year it would have been appropriate if the meeting could have been staged at its original home, Wembley.

Not surprisingly, the Polish fans were hoping for a home champion, but Ivan Mauger had already drummed out a warning by winning the European title in Russia a few weeks before, while Barrry Briggs was still a danger, Anders Michanek was in scintillating form, and newcomer Ole Olsen had been upsetting many established names.

On a windy afternoon, the 50,000 crowd at the stadium were anticipating some hectic action on a track with a strangely black racing surface. They certainly got what they wanted in heat one when Antoni Woryna was a popular winner. Michanek showed well early in the race, but was eventually relegated to last position, a performance that virtually ended his championship hopes. Heat two saw a meeting of four world final debutants — Olsen, Trevor Hedge, Russian Valeri Gordeev and Pole Zygfryd Friedek. Hedge suffered machine trouble, while Olsen won his first world final ride and Friedek fell, leaving Gordeev as the only other finisher.

Mauger, Briggs and the experienced Russian Gennady Kurilenko met in the third heat, but Poland's Jan Mucha proved the surprise package as he worried Briggs after Mauger had made another jet-like start — Kurilenko fell on the first lap. Polish cheers resounded again in heat four, which saw Pawel Waloszek winning from Soren Sjosten. Woryna won his second

Ivan Mauger (right) rode to his third consecutive world title in 1970, while Pole Jan Mucha could score only six points.

race in heat five from a sound Mucha, while Valeri Klementiev looked ill at ease and Hedge petered out with more engine problems.

Heat six looked like an easy win for Mauger, but Henryk Glucklich made him work hard for his victory, and Gordeev also made a late but unsuccessful challenge. Heat seven was an entertaining race, with East German Hans Jurgen Fritz making a good start, only to be passed by his three rivals. Sjosten moved into the lead, but Olsen first had to pass Briggs to get on terms with the Swede. By the time he reached second place, however, he was too late to worry Sjosten.

Waloszek won his second race when he disposed of Klementiev and Michanek in heat eight, and his title chances looked even better after heat nine, in which he came out again to beat his buddy Woryna in the fastest time of the night. Meanwhile Briggs had a rare battle with Gordeev for third position, only to come off worse.

Heat 10 brought a nasty-looking pile-up as Glucklich and Kurilenko tangled, bringing down the luckless Hedge, who was unfit to ride in the re-run. Glucklich was lucky not to have been excluded for his part in this incident, but took full advantage of his fortune to win the re-run from Edmund Migos, the reserve who had taken Hedge's place.

The next race brought four top names to the line in Mauger, Olsen, Michanek and Klementiev. Almost inevitably, Mauger made the gate, but engine trouble robbed Olsen of second place, allowing Michanek to take over. Mauger and Waloszek remained unbeaten after each had had three races, and Woryna, only one point behind, and Glucklich on seven, underlined the Polish challenge. The crowd was anticipating heat 15, when the two unbeaten men would meet.

Meanwhile Woryna won heat 13, but Olsen was plagued with mechanical problems for the second consecutive race. Heat 14 produced another bad spill when Friedek went down, breaking an arm. But the race was not stopped even though the Pole was still lying on the track, and among the survivors Klementiev and Gordeev kept Briggs in third place.

Now for the big one — Mauger against Waloszek. The battered Hedge reappeared for this race, if only in an attempt to stop Waloszek's team-mate Migos from interfering in matters. But in this event Mauger made another of his superb starts and won the race in untroubled fashion. Waloszek remained in contention, however, by filling second place.

Sjosten won heat 16 from Michanek, and then in the next race Mauger squared up to the other top Pole, Woryna. Another dynamic start by Mauger settled matters almost immediately, however, and made him

Antoni Woryna gained a fine 13 points in the last of his five world final appearances.

Trevor Hedge failed to score in 1970, but was England's sole representative.

the first rider to win the world championship in three consecutive years. He had also achieved his hat-trick in three different countries, a record that will be difficult for any rider to beat.

The rest of the programme now appeared almost a formality, with Waloszek winning the 18th heat to secure the runner-up placing, Klementiev taking the 19th heat, and Briggs riding to victory in the finale from Michanek.

Amid all the jubilation for Mauger's achievement there were probably few who spared a thought for the luckless Trevor Hedge. As England's only representative in this event, he had maintained his country's proud record of having a rider in every world final staged up to that time, yet his no-score return was an injustice to a man who had promised so much, but had been robbed through no fault of his own. Even less fortunate was Russian Yuri Dubinin, who had qualified for the final but was forced to miss it when he suffered a broken thigh.

Score Chart

								Total
1 Ivan Mauger	New Zealand	3	3	3	3	3		15
2 Pawel Waloszek	Poland	3	3	3	2	3		14
3 Antoni Woryna	Poland	3	3	2	3	2		13
4 Soren Sjosten	Sweden	2	3	1	3	f		9
Henryk Glucklich	Poland	2	2	3	2	f/r		9
6 Valeri Klementiev	USSR	0	1	1	3	3		8
7 Barry Briggs	New Zealand	2	1	0	1	3		7
Andrzej Wyglenda	Poland	1	0	3	2	1		7
Anders Michanek	Sweden	0	1	2	2	2		7
10 Ole Olsen	Denmark	3	2	0	ef	1		6
Jan Mucha	Poland	1	2	0	1	2		6
12 Hans Jurgen Fritz	E Germany	1	0	1	1	2		5
Valeri Gordeev	USSR	2	1	1	0	1		5
14 Gennady Kurilenko	USSR	f	2	f/e	ns	ns		2
Zygfryd Friedek	Poland	f	0	2	f	ns		2
16 Trevor Hedge	England	ef	0	f	ret	ns		0
Edmund Migos (res)	Poland	2	1	1	f	0		4
Jerzy Szczakiel (res)	Poland	(did not ride)						

Heat-by-heat

		Time
1	Woryna, Glucklich, Fritz, Michanek	77.8s
2	Olsen, Gordeev, Hedge (ef), Friedek (f)	78.3s
3	Mauger, Briggs, Mucha, Kurilenko (f)	77.3s
4	Waloszek, Sjosten, Wyglenda, Klementiev	77.4s
5	Woryna, Mucha, Klementiev, Hedge (ef)	77.6s
6	Mauger, Glucklich, Gordeev, Wyglenda	77.6s
7	Sjosten, Olsen, Briggs, Fritz	78.2s
8	Waloszek, Kurilenko, Michanek, Friedek	77.5s
9	Waloszek, Woryna, Gordeev, Briggs	77.1s
10	Glucklich, Migos, Sjosten, Kurilenko (f/exc), Hedge (f)	77.8s
11	Wyglenda, Friedek, Fritz, Mucha	78.5s
12	Mauger, Michanek, Klementiev, Olsen	77.7s
13	Woryna, Wyglenda, Migos, Olsen (ef)	77.8s
14	Klementiev, Glucklich, Briggs, Friedek (f)	78.2s
15	Mauger, Waloszek, Fritz, Hedge (ret)	77.9s
16	Sjosten, Michanek, Mucha, Gordeev	78.8s
17	Mauger, Woryna, Migos (ret), Sjosten (f)	77.6s
18	Waloszek, Mucha, Olsen, Glucklich (f/re)	78.2s
19	Klementiev, Fritz, Gordeev, Migos (f)	79.6s
20	Briggs, Michanek, Wyglenda, Migos	78.1s

Pawel Waloszek gave Poland a fine second place overall on the first occasion a world final was staged in his country.

Russian Valeri Klementiev supported the Eastern cause with an eight-point score that included two heat wins.

1971 Swedish hopes crash

SO FAR Sweden had not been able to supply a winner on the three occasions that the world final had been staged at the Ullevi track in Gothenburg. But when the event returned to Sweden in 1971, the home crowd had high hopes of a victory from either Anders Michanek or Bernt Persson. Whatever the destination of the championship, one record was broken this season — for the first time in 18 years Barry Briggs was missing from a world final.

Very much in evidence, however, was Ivan Mauger. The world champion for the past three years was the undoubted favourite again, even though he had earlier lost his European title to his protege, Ole Olsen, at Wembley. Russian hopes rested on newcomer Vladimir Gordeev — brother of former finalist Valeri — while another promising newcomer was Poland's Jerzy Szczakiel. Another feature of this final was the appearance of the brothers Boocock; not since 1953 when Fred and Eric Williams had raced at Wembley had two members of the same family ridden together in a final.

The 32,000 crowd was surprised when Ray Wilson won the first heat from Michanek, but Mauger made no mistake in the second, beating Jim Airey and Gordeev. Airey was the first Australian to ride in a world final since 1963. The Swedish fans at last had something to cheer in heat three when Persson and Soren Sjosten beat Ronnie Moore, but the home

fortunes were reversed in the next race when Denmark's Olsen beat Bengt and the late Tommy Jansson (who, incidentally, were not related).

Bengt Jansson made amends, however, by taking the fifth heat from Nigel Boocock. In the next race Olsen started badly and it took him three laps to reach the front. Once there, however, he had no difficulty in winning from Moore and Jiri Stancl, Eric Boocock finishing in last place for the second time. There was drama in the seventh heat when Szczakiel fell, bumping Mauger as he went down on the first turn. Mauger lost valuable time before he could regain control and was unable to get past the rapid Wilson and Sjosten. This third placing could well have cost Mauger the title, as it transpired later in the evening.

In heat eight the impressive Gordeev beat three Swedish riders, Michanek, Persson, and Tommy Jansson, and heat nine produced another upset for the fans when Eric Boocock at last pulled his form together to win easily from Sjosten, with Nigel Boocock in third place. Heat 10 was a procession, with Airey leading from Persson. The next race brought together Olsen, Wilson, and Gordeev, and the unfancied Swedish rider Leif Enecrona. But it was Enecrona who was at the centre of the excitement, when the race was stopped and a lengthy dispute took place as to whether or not the Swede had broken the tapes. This row had an unfortunate effect on the suspect temperament of Wilson.

Ole Olsen clinches the world title in his last race of the night by beating Soren Sjosten (centre) and Anders Michanek (left).

who was unable to get on terms in the re-run, in which Olsen was the winner from Gordeev in the fastest time of the night. Mauger won heat 12 from Michanek, and at the three-ride stage Olsen led with an unbeaten nine points, Wilson and Mauger had seven each, and Michanek, Gordeev, Persson, Airey, Sjosten and Bengt Jansson were bunched on the six-point mark.

He looked even more like lifting the championship when he beat Mauger in the 13th heat. Gordeev went down to Bengt Jansson in the 14th, and Wilson beat Airey in the next race to sort out the contest for the minor placings a little. Michanek won the 16th heat, and Gordeev took the next race to finish the night with 11 points. Giving himself a chance to get among the top three, Mauger won heat 18 to get a final total of 12 points, but a crucial race in the struggle for second and third placings overall was heat 19. Wilson and Bengt Jansson each needed to win it to tie with Mauger on 12 points, but once again the Englishman's nerves seemed to play a part, when he gated first, only to be

Olsen makes his first appearance on a world final rostrum sandwiched by Ivan Mauger and Bengt Jansson (right).

Ray Wilson jets away from Russians Grigori Chlynovski and Vladimir Gordeev in the European final at Wembley. He finished joint fourth in the world final.

an Mauger wins heat 12 from Anders Michanek on the
levi track.

passed by Jansson and Persson within a lap. Persson was content to let his countryman streak ahead and appeared to concentrate on keeping Wilson back in third place, a job that gave him no trouble.

Olsen needed only one point to be sure of the title in heat 20, and even if he fell or suffered engine trouble he would get the chance of a run-off with Mauger. But Olsen made no mistakes, winning from Michanek, Sjosten, and Airey to become the first Danish World Speedway Champion. In doing so he had ruined Mauger's hopes of making it four world titles in a row, but the reception that Olsen received from the crowd made it evident that he was one of the most popular of world final winners.

The run-off for second place turned into a mere formality when Mauger made the gate and led Jansson home. Later, after the initial drama of the evening had been forgotten, Gordeev was accused of using illegal fuel and given a year's suspension, a decision that raised Wilson to fourth place overall.

Score Chart

									Total
1	Ole Olsen	Denmark	3	3	3	3	3	15
2	Ivan Mauger	New Zealand	3	1	3	2	3	12
3	Bengt Jansson	Sweden	2	3	1	3	3	12
4	Ray Wilson	England	3	3	1	3	1	11
	Vladimir Gordeev	USSR	1	3	2	2	3	11
	Anders Michanek	Sweden	2	2	2	3	2	11
7	Bernt Persson	Sweden	3	1	2	1	2	9
8	Jim Airey	Australia	2	1	3	2	0	8
	Soren Sjosten	Sweden	2	2	1	1	8	
10	Nigel Boocock	England	1	2	1	0	2	6
11	Eric Boocock	England	0	0	3	1	0	4
	Ronnie Moore	New Zealand	1	2	0	0	1	4
	Leif Enecrona	Sweden	0	0	0	2	2	4
14	Jiri Stancl	Czechoslovakia	0	1	1	0	1	3
15	Tommy Jansson	Sweden	1	0	0	0	0	1
16	Jerzy Szczakiel	Poland	0	f	0	0	0	0
	Gote Nordin (res)	Sweden	(did not ride)					
	Tony Lomas (res)	England	(did not ride)					

Heat-by-heat

		Time
1	Wilson, Michanek, N Boocock, Stancl	78.6s
2	Mauger, Airey, Vladimir Gordeev, E Boocock	80.5s
3	Persson, Sjosten, Moore, Enecrona	79.8s
4	Olsen, B Jansson, T Jansson, Szczakiel	78.8s
5	B Jansson, N Boocock, Airey, Enecrona	80.3s
6	Olsen, Moore, Stancl, E Boocock	80.0s
7	Wilson, Sjosten, Mauger, Szczakiel	80.4s
8	Vladimir Gordeev, Michanek, Persson, T Jansson	79.6s
9	E Boocock, Sjosten, N Boocock, T Jansson	80.5s
10	Airey, Persson, Stancl, Szczakiel	80.4s
11	Olsen, Vladimir Gordeev, Wilson, Enecrona	78.4s
12	Mauger, Michanek, B Jansson, Moore	80.2s
13	Olsen, Mauger, Persson, N Boocock	79.8s
14	B Jansson, Vladimir Gordeev, Sjosten, Stancl	79.4s
15	Wilson, Airey, Moore, T Jansson	80.3s
16	Michanek, Enecrona, E Boocock, Szczakiel	80.8s
17	Vladimir Gordeev, N Boocock, Moore, Szczakiel	80.3s
18	Mauger, Enecrona, Stancl, T Jansson	80.9s
19	B Jansson, Persson, Wilson, E Boocock	80.6s
20	Olsen, Michanek, Sjosten, Airey	80.5s
21	Mauger beat B Jansson in run-off for 2nd place.	79.8s

m Airey rode to a solid eight points in the sole world final
ppearance of his career.

1972
Master of the run-off

SPEEDWAY PURISTS suggest that the world final should always be held at its original home at Wembley, and thus they were happy when the event returned there in 1972. But such had been the international growth of the sport that it became evident to most observers that from now on Wembley would be lucky in staging the final only at intervals of three or four years.

From the usual crop of qualifying rounds Ivan Mauger emerged as British champion, and was joined at Wembley by the next four highest home-based scorers. The European champion was the near-veteran Pawel Waloszek, and also present at Wembley were reigning world champion Ole Olsen, six Russian riders, and three Swedes.

Almost 80,000 fans expected a battle for the title between the two great rivals and friends, Olsen and Mauger. However, with the half-dozen Russians in the line-up it was possible that they might arrange some 'team riding' that could affect the final outcome. As it happened, the night started in drama and turned out to be arguably the most exciting final yet seen.

Heat one had to be re-run no less than three times after falls, tape breakages and general confusion delayed the outcome for 15 minutes. Waloszek was the eventual winner from Russian newcomer Grigori Chlynovski, while Anders Michanek and Eric Boocock were the unlucky victims of crashes. Mauger's hopes took a jolt in heat two when he was beaten by Briggs. In heat three Nigel Boocock had to contend with three Russians, but managed to finish second to Anatoli Kuzmin.

In heat four it was the turn of the other highly rated rider, Olsen, to experience downfall. He and John Louis tangled on the first bend, the mix-up knocking Olsen back into last place. Recovering determination, Olsen went after Louis and passed him into third place on the second lap, and next time round he overtook Bernt Persson. Going like an express train, Olsen clearly decided to risk all for the chance of victory, and attempted to ride round the outside of race leader Christer Lofqvist. But in doing so he gave the bike too much throttle, and went down as a fallen champion in more senses than one.

Further tragedy occurred in heat five, and ended in Barry Briggs being rushed to hospital, where he had to have a finger amputated. Persson, Briggs and Valeri

A bad year for accidents: Alexander Pavlov falls in front of Bernt Persson in heat 12 (top), Barry Briggs goes down in heat five (above), and Pawel Waloszek and Eric Boocock (right) tangle in heat one (below).

British final action: Ivan Mauger leads (from left) John Louis, Trevor Hedge and Gary Middleton.

Gordeev raced into the first bend in a line. Briggs and Persson emerged together, with the Russian just behind. But then Briggs appeared to lose control just as Persson was fighting his own machine on the exit from the turn. They touched and Briggs went down, to be hit from behind by Gordeev, whose machine careered along the track, climbed the safety fence, and came to rest on the greyhound track. Briggs was taken off on a stretcher, and Persson won the re-run from reserve Jan Simensen, with a shaken Gordeev in last place.

Mauger made a flying start in heat six to win from Louis, Russian Alexander Pavlov took the next race, and heats eight and nine both went to Olsen, who was riding aggressively in the hope of salvaging something from the night's racing after his earlier fall. As a measure of his determination, he won heat eight in the fastest time of the night, and easily beat none other than Mauger in the ninth.

Heat 10 saw reserve Jim McMillan take the place of the injured Briggs, and in so doing he became only the second Scottish rider to appear in a world final (Ken McKinlay had been the first). Lofqvist won the race from Nigel Boocock. British fans were happy to see Louis out in front in heat 11, when Russians Viktor Trofimov and Gordeev indulged in some pushing and shoving at the expense of Waloszek, who fell.

85

Sweden's Christer Lofqvist enjoyed a brilliant world final debut in 1972, finishing joint fourth overall with an 11-point total that included three heat wins.

Persson, who had benefitted from Briggs' disappearance by winning the re-run of heat five, was in luck again in race 12 when Pavlov fell while comfortably in the lead. Pavlov recovered to win the next race, however, and Persson won the 14th with the aid of a jet-like start. Olsen won heat 15 after a tight race with yet another of the Russians, Viktor Kalmykov, and Mauger stamped his authority on the meeting by taking heat 16 after Lofqvist had overcooked things on the first turn.

Lofqvist bounced back to win the next heat, ending the night with an 11-point score that could have been so much better but for his solitary last place. Olsen missed the gate in heat 18, but picked the opposition off one by one much to the enjoyment of the crowd. Heat 19 was to be vital in deciding the outcome of the night's racing, as it included the two top scorers so far, Mauger and Persson. Mauger needed to win the heat to enforce a run-off with Persson for the championship; he held up proceedings while he inspected the track and the starting area, but then he gated as only Mauger can, to lead all the way. Meanwhile Persson had to fight past Waloszek before he could take second place and guarantee that a run-off would be needed. In the last heat Louis scored his second win of the night to take joint fourth overall after five consistent rides.

In the run-off for the title, it took Mauger longer to inspect the track and starting area again than it did for him to win the race. But it wasn't that easy — Persson endured a constant peppering with shale from the leader's rear wheel, but still managed a final fling on the last turn that must have surprised Mauger. Olsen was placed third overall, after a tremendous night of tension-packed racing.

Score Chart

								Total
1	Ivan Mauger	New Zealand	2	3	2	3	3	13
2	Bernt Persson	Sweden	2	3	3	3	2	13
3	Ole Olsen	Denmark	f	3	3	3	3	12
4	Christer Lofqvist	Sweden	3	2	3	0	3	11
	John Louis	England	1	2	3	2	3	11
6	Alexander Pavlov	USSR	1	3	f	3	1	8
	Anders Michanek	Sweden	f/e	2	2	2	2	8
8	Pawel Waloszek	Poland	3	1	f	1	1	6
	Viktor Trofimov	USSR	0	f	2	2	2	6
	Nigel Boocock	England	2	1	2	1	0	6
	Viktor Kalmykov	USSR	1	1	1	2	1	6
12	Anatoli Kuzmin	USSR	3	0	0	1	0	4
	Grigori Chlynovski	USSR	2	1	1	0	0	4
14	Barry Briggs	New Zealand	3	f	ns	ns	ns	3
15	Eric Boocock	England	f/e	0	0	0	2	2
	Valeri Gordeev	USSR	0	0	1	0	2	2
	Jan Simensen	Sweden (res)		2		0		2
	Jim McMillan	Scotland (res)			1		1	2

Heat-by-heat

		Time
1	Waloszek, Chlynovski, Michanek (f/exc), E Boocock (f)	72.2s
2	Briggs, Mauger, Pavlov, Trofimov	70.4s
3	Kuzmin, N Boocock, Kalmykov, Gordeev	71.4s
4	Lofqvist, Persson, Louis, Olsen (f/ret)	71.0s
5	Persson, Simensen, Chlynovski, Gordeev, Briggs (f)	69.2s
6	Mauger, Louis, Kalmykov, E Boocock	70.2s
7	Pavlov, Lofqvist, Waloszek, Kuzmin	70.6s
8	Olsen, Michanek, N Boocock, Trofimov (f/ret)	69.8s
9	Olsen, Mauger, Chlynovski, Kuzmin	70.4s
10	Lofqvist, N Boocock, McMillan, E Boocock	71.4s
11	Louis, Trofimov, Gordeev, Waloszek (f)	70.4s
12	Persson, Michanek, Kalmykov, Pavlov (f)	70.2s
13	Pavlov, Louis, N Boocock, Chlynovski	71.2s
14	Persson, Trofimov, Kuzmin, E Boocock	70.0s
15	Olsen, Kalmykov, Waloszek, Simensen	71.0s
16	Mauger, Michanek, Gordeev, Lofqvist	71.0s
17	Lofqvist, Trofimov, Kalmykov, Chlynovski	71.4s
18	Olsen, E Boocock, Pavlov, Gordeev	71.2s
19	Mauger, Persson, Waloszek, N Boocock	71.0s
20	Louis, Michanek, McMillan, Kuzmin	71.2s
21	Mauger beat Persson in run-off for 1st place	70.2s

1973 Year of the unknown Pole

Poland's first world champion, Jerzy Szczakiel, heads for the finish line in front of Zenon Plech and Jan Mucha.

THIS SEASON the world final returned to Poland, with the Slaski stadium in Katowice being the venue. And while British, Scandinavian, and Continental contestants went through the usual qualifying procedures, Polish riders were declared exempt from these. Instead their five leading riders were nominated to appear in the final with the successful qualifiers from other countries, who consisted of four Russians, two Britons, two Swedes, and lone representatives from New Zealand, Australia, and Denmark.

The partisan 95,000 crowd had arrived to see a Polish world champion, and it was obvious from the condition of the track that the home riders had been practising with that aim in view. When visiting riders inspected the track the day before the final they found the surface in an atrocious condition, and concern was expressed about this and about the West German referee, who had been responsible for some disputed decisions at Wembley the previous year.

Racing started in unexciting fashion with Russian Vladimir Paxnikov winning heat one, as Anders Michanek slumped to last place. Heat two brought an early clash of title pretenders, but Ivan Mauger sped from the gate to win from one of the home riders, Zenon Plech, while Ole Olsen and Ray Wilson tangled at the back, the latter falling.

Heat four gave the crowd something to cheer about as Edward Jancarz beat Valeri Gordeev, but a crash by Russian Vladimir Zapleczny gave some indication of the treacherous track conditions. There was yet another fall in the fourth heat as Bernt Persson went down while chasing popular winner Jerzy Szczakiel. Michanek won heat five, and a battle between Wilson and world final newcomer Peter Collins was resolved when Jancarz came from the back to relegate Collins to last place. Plech took the sixth from another new boy, John Boulger, but Olsen started badly in the next race and pulled up to second place as Grigori Chlynovski won.

Mauger made a rare poor start in heat eight, and finished a lowly third after unsuccessfully attempting to split the home pairing of Szczakiel and Pawel Waloszek. Then Szczakiel went out again to win the ninth heat from Plech, a performance that gave him three wins from three starts. Michanek was excluded for breaking the tapes in this race, a refereeing decision that was erratic, as several other riders had already committed some sort of offence on the start line without being penalised.

Wilson showed the Russians Paznikov and Gordeev the way home in heat 10, but Persson suffered engine failure and had to withdraw from the meeting as he had no spare machine. Mauger made another botch of the start in heat 11, but this time he was able to catch Boulger and Chlynovski. In this race the tapes had been broken four times without any rider being excluded, and they were parted again in the next heat when Olsen won from Collins, who was beginning to adapt to the strange conditions. After all riders had had three outings, Szczakiel had emerged as clear favourite for the title, as his closest pursuers, Plech, Mauger, and Chlynovski, had each dropped two points.

Fast-gating Gordeev put one over Olsen in heat 13, but in third and fourth places Michanek and Boulger looked decidedly uncomfortable. Heat 14 was restarted after the tapes had again been broken with no rider being penalised, and in the re-run Mauger won from the gate. Heat 15 brought Szczakiel's first defeat, Chlynovski passing him on the first turn and increasing his lead on every lap.

Heat 16 was an all-Polish affair and looked like a decidedly 'arranged' race as Plech, a potential winner of the championship, took the flag from Jancarz. Then Mauger beat Michanek in the 17th heat to finish with a 13-point total. He now needed Szczakiel to drop another point if there was to be run-off for the title, and Mauger's friend Olsen duly obliged by beating the Pole in the next heat.

Heat 19 was also crucial — if either Plech or Chlynovski won he would join Mauger and Szczakiel in the run-off. A good gate by Collins was nullified by Plech, who ran into him on the first lap. Chlynovski and Gordeev rode by the bewildered Collins, but on the last lap Chlynovski attempted to slide under Plech and brought the Pole down. Chlynovski was excluded and a re-run was ordered, although the referee had neglected to halt the race when Collins was originally

Ivan Mauger sweeps round the outside of Jan Mucha (centre) and Vladimir Paznikov in heat 14. But Mauger's error in the run-off gave Eastern Europe its first world champion.

barged. After arguments that lasted half an hour it was eventually decided that the race positions that held at the time of the Collins-Plech encounter would stand. Thus Collins was declared the race winner from Plech and Gordeev. This assured Plech of third place overall, much to the annoyance of Olsen, who had scored 11 points the hard way.

In the run-off for the title, Szczakiel beat Mauger out of the gate. But instead of waiting for the 24-year-old Pole to make a mistake, Mauger tried to go inside on the pits turn. He clipped his opponent's rear wheel and was thrown over his handlebars, and thus a rider who was almost unknown to Western speedway followers became Poland's first world champion.

Score Chart

								Total
1	Jerzy Szczakiel	Poland	3	3	3	2	2	13
2	Ivan Mauger	New Zealand	3	1	3	3	3	13
3	Zenon Plech	Poland	2	3	2	3	2	12
4	Ole Olsen	Denmark	1	2	3	2	3	11
5	Grigori Chlynovski	USSR	2	3	2	3	exc	10
6	Vladimir Paznikov	USSR	3	1	2	1	1	8
	Pawel Waloszek	Poland	1	2	1	1	3	8
8	Valeri Gordeev	USSR	2	0	1	3	1	7
	Jan Mucha	Poland	1	1	1	2	2	7
10	Anders Michanek	Sweden	0	3	exc	1	2	6
	Edward Jancarz	Poland	3	1	0	2	0	6
	Peter Collins	England	1	0	2	0	3	6
	John Boulger	Australia	2	2	1	0	1	6
14	Ray Wilson	England	f	2	3	0	f	5
15	Vladimir Zapleczny	USSR	0	0	0	1	1	2
16	Bernt Persson	Sweden	f	0	ret	ns	ns	0
	Andrzej Wyglenda (res)	Poland				0		0
	Tommy Jansson (res)	Sweden					0	0
	Henryk Zyto (res)	Poland	(did not ride)					

Heat-by-heat

		Time
1	Paznikov, Chlynovski, Waloszek, Michanek	80.8s
2	Mauger, Plech, Olsen, Wilson (f)	80.2s
3	Jancarz, Gordeev, Mucha, Zapleczny (f/re)	81.5s
4	Szczakiel, Boulger, Collins, Persson (f)	81.2s
5	Michanek, Wilson, Jancarz, Collins	80.4s
6	Plech, Boulger, Paznikov, Zapleczny	80.8s
7	Chlynovski, Olsen, Mucha, Persson	80.4s
8	Szczakiel, Waloszek, Mauger, Gordeev	81.0s
9	Szczakiel, Plech, Mucha, Michanek (exc)	80.7s
10	Wilson, Paznikov, Gordeev, Persson (ret)	80.2s
11	Mauger, Chlynovski, Boulger, Jancarz	80.4s
12	Olsen, Collins, Waloszek, Zapleczny	81.4s
13	Gordeev, Olsen, Michanek, Boulger	80.6s
14	Mauger, Mucha, Paznikov, Collins	80.2s
15	Chlynovski, Szczakiel, Zapleczny, Wilson	80.6s
16	Plech, Jancarz, Waloszek, Wyglenda	80.8s
17	Mauger, Michanek, Zapleczny, Jansson	80.8s
18	Olsen, Szczakiel, Paznikov, Jancarz	80.2s
19	Collins, Plech, Gordeev, Chlynovski (exc)	no time
20	Waloszek, Mucha, Boulger, Wilson (f)	80.6s
21	Szczakiel beat Mauger in run-off for 1st place	no time

After the most unexpected win in world final history, Szczakiel accepts the winner's laurels, while Ivan Mauger looks ruefully on.

The two highest scoring Russians at Katowice, Vladimir Paznikov (leading) and Grigori Chlynovski, blaze away from Anders Michanek.

1974
Michanek's 'record' night

WITH THE PREVIOUS season providing a home rider as winner when the world final was held in Poland, Swedish fans were hoping for a similar ending to the 1974 event, which returned to the Ullevi stadium in Gothenburg. Five Swedish riders had qualified, together with 11 riders from the European Final. Rain had swamped the track in the two days previous to the final, and every effort had been made to dry it out for the big occasion, including the use of a jet-engined car which projected heated air on to the surface.

As early as heat one the 39,000 crowd had an excuse to celebrate when home rider Christer Lofqvist passed the fast-gating Ivan Mauger to win, setting a new track record in the process. The record was chipped away by a further fifth of a second when Tommy Johansson won heat two, and Bengt Jansson had to work hard to reach second place by passing Grigori Chlynovski and Terry Betts.

Heat three provided a hint of the way the night's racing was to develop when Ole Olsen and Dag Lovaas were first away, but Anders Michanek was leading by the time they blasted out of the first turn. In yet another record-breaking race, Michanek carved a whole second off the previous best set by Johansson. Behind him, Olsen took second place while Lovaas kept the Pole Zenon Plech in last place.

Sweden's Soren Sjosten was challenged by the English trio of John Louis, Peter Collins and Dave Jessup in heat four, but still managed to come out on top. Collins made a mess of his gating and had to pass his two countrymen, but was unable to catch the flying Swede. Sjosten came straight out again to contest an eventful heat five, which featured potential champions Mauger and Olsen. Mauger made his customary flying start, but sadly for him the race was stopped when Olsen and Betts tangled with the tapes. In the re-run Sjosten broke into the lead, with Mauger and Olsen in pursuit. Olsen tried to ride round Mauger but fell, suffering a chipped shin bone and retiring from the meeting. Sjosten maintained the pressure to keep Mauger in second place. Then Michanek went out to make it six Swedish victories in the first six races, breaking the track record yet again.

Heat seven brought another crash, when Johansson was forced out on the first turn and was hit by Russian Vladimir Gordeev. Gordeev was taken off by stretcher with an injured shoulder, and the incident obviously had an effect on Johansson, who finished last in the

A proud Anders Michanek after his unbeaten night in the Ullevi stadium.

re-run behind Plech, Collins and reserve Tommy Jansson. Louis came up against two Swedes in heat eight, but to prove they could be beaten he led easily all the way. Louis reappeared in heat nine, but this time he finished last behind Mauger, Chlynovski and Plech after gating in second place. Another poor start by Collins in heat ten cost him a much needed point as he chased winner Lovaas in vain.

Bengt Jansson maintained the Swedish pressure by winning heat 11, and the next race matched four of the five home riders together. But the competition seemed to have no effect on Michanek's nerves, as he streaked from the gate and led all the way, breaking the track record for the third time. While he remained the only unbeaten rider, Sjosten was relegated to third place by Lofqvist. With Michanek now on nine points, Lofqvist, Mauger, and Sjosten had seven, and Collins and Bengt Jansson were on six.

Mauger dropped another point in heat 13, this time to Johansson, while Lovaas and Jessup finished third and fourth. Bengt Jansson gated in front of Sjosten in heat 14, but the man who forced the pace was Plech, who put in three-and-a-half laps of daredevil riding. At the flag he was in second place behind Jansson, and still on his bike, much to the surprise of the crowd. Sjosten's third place meant that his slim chance of the title had now disappeared completely.

Michanek displays the immaculate style that took him to his 1974 championship.

The dynamic Pole Zenon Plech gets wildly out of control as he chases Bengt Jansson.

Soren Sjosten (left) makes a better start in the run-off, but Ivan Mauger won the race.

The English duo of John Louis and Dave Jessup (right) pursue the flying Soren Sjosten.

Heat 15 saw Anders 'Super-Mich' win as he pleased once again, taking a three-point lead over his closest challengers for the title. Collins, who had won the European championship at the age of 20 shortly before this world final, tried to emulate Plech's razor-edge tactics in heat 16 when he passed Lofqvist and all but beat Chlynovski, who showed track craft as well as speed in keeping the young Englishman at bay.

Michanek needed only a single point when he came out for his last race in heat 17, but he took three when he beat not only the four-times world champion Mauger but also the new European king, Collins. As the first Swedish rider to win the title since Ove Fundin in 1967, and only the second Swede to win on a home track, Michanek was rightly accorded a tremendous welcome by the crowd.

Louis scored his second win of the meeting in heat 18, beating Johansson and Russian Mikhail Krasnov. Sjosten needed a win in the next heat to enforce a run-off for second place overall with Mauger, but was up against the improving Chlynovski. But Sjosten made no mistake, leading from the gate while Chlynovski seemed a different rider from the inspired man who had out-ridden Collins just a couple of races ago, and eventually crashed out of the running. Lofqvist could have earned himself a place in the run-off if he had won his last outing in heat 20, but instead he finished last as Betts scored a heat win in his world final debut.

Remembering his disaster of the previous year at Katowice when he crashed in a run-off for the world title, Mauger made no mistake in this year's decider for second place overall, leading Sjosten from the gate. And, making only his second appearance in a world final, John Louis was accorded fourth place overall, even though he tied on points with Bengt Jansson and Collins, on the basis of heat wins, second places, winning times, and the results when the three riders met during the meeting.

Score Chart

								Total
1 Anders Michanek	Sweden	3	3	3	3	3	15
2 Ivan Mauger	New Zealand	2	2	3	2	2	11
3 Soren Sjosten	Sweden	3	3	1	1	3	11
4 John Louis	England	1	3	0	2	3	9
Bengt Jansson	Sweden	2	1	3	3	ret	9
Peter Collins	England	2	2	2	2	1	9
7 Tommy Johansson	Sweden	3	0	0	3	2	8
Zenon Plech	Poland	0	3	1	2	2	8
Christer Lofqvist	Sweden	3	2	2	1	ret	8
10 Grigori Chlynovski	USSR	1	0	2	3	f	6
Dag Lovaas	Norway	1	0	3	1	1	6
Terry Betts	England	0	1	1	1	3	6
13 Dave Jessup	England	0	2	2	0	1	5
14 Mikhail Krasnov	USSR	1	1	ret	0	1	3
15 Ole Olsen	Denmark	2	f	ns	ns	ns	2
16 Vladimir Gordeev	USSR	0	f	ns	ns	ns	0
Tommy Jansson (res)	·Sweden			1	0	2	3
Edward Jancarz (res)	Poland			1	0	ret	1

NB: 4th and subsequent places were decided by working out heat wins, second places, winning times and the results when tied riders met during the meeting.

Heat-by-heat

		Time
1	Lofqvist, Mauger, Krasnov, Gordeev	74.7s
2	Johansson, B Jansson, Chlynovski, Betts	74.5s
3	Michanek, Olsen, Lovaas, Plech	73.5s
4	Sjosten, Collins, Louis, Jessup	75.3s
5	Sjosten, Mauger, Betts, Olsen (f)	75.7s
6	Michanek, Jessup, Krasnov, Chlynovski	73.1s
7	Plech, Collins, T Jansson, Johansson, Gordeev (f/exc)	74.2s
8	Louis, Lofqvist, B Jansson, Lovaas	74.6s
9	Mauger, Chlynovski, Plech, Louis	75.1s
10	Lovaas, Collins, Betts, Krasnov (ret)	74.6s
11	B Jansson, Jessup, Jancarz (Olsen & Gordeev ns)	74.6s
12	Michanek, Lofqvist, Sjosten, Johansson	72.8s
13	Johansson, Mauger, Lovaas, Jessup	75.0s
14	B Jansson, Plech, Sjosten, Krasnov	74.5s
15	Michanek, Louis, Betts, Jancarz	73.5s
16	Chlynovski, Collins, Lofqvist, T Jansson	75.8s
17	Michanek, Mauger, Collins, B Jansson (ret)	74.5s
18	Louis, Johansson, Krasnov, Jancarz (ret)	74.0s
19	Sjosten, T Jansson, Lovaas, Chlynovski (f)	76.0s
20	Betts, Plech, Jessup, Lofqvist (ret)	75.0s
21	Mauger beat Sjosten in run-off for 2nd place	75.0s

1975 Olsen's clean sweep

FOR MANY speedway followers, the world finals of the two previous seasons had not assumed the lustre usually associated with this showcase event. It was not that the Polish or Swedish authorities lacked anything in presentation or expertise, but the simple fact remains that when the world final is staged at Wembley stadium the atmosphere is unique. No other venue is able to summon the tension and sense of climax as does the traditional home of world championship speedway, and thus it was no surprise when 85,000 spectators paid record receipts of £150,000 to watch the 1975 event. Not even the threat of a bomb scare, which turned out to be a hoax, sent them from the stadium when it was announced half-way through the meeting.

Even the aura of Wembley, however, could not prevent riders from criticising the state of the track when they practised on it on the Thursday before the final. And the rough condition of the oval came in for still more abuse when the top four British-based riders and the highest-scoring 12 from the European final met on the Saturday night.

As early as the first turn in the first race Australian Phil Crump hit a bump, forcing Bernt Persson wide and allowing Edward Jancarz and Valeri Gordeev through. Crump recovered magnificently, however, to win his debut ride in a world final. Ivan Mauger won the second heat from Malcolm Simmons, while Tommy Jansson pushed an out-of-touch Ray Wilson into last place.

English hopes rose in the third heat when Peter Collins took John Louis on the first lap to win handsomely. At the back, Zenon Plech won a battle for third place with fellow Pole Henryk Glucklich. In heat four Ole Olsen passed the fast-gating Viktor Trofimov at the end of lap one, but Anders Michanek's hopes took a dive when he was unable to follow through and dropped two points. Heat five saw Crump in winning form again, with Simmons also riding well as he passed Plech and Marek Ceislak from the back.

Mauger made the rare mistake of missing the gate in heat six, allowing Olsen to break into a winning lead. Then Louis got past Mauger to put the Kiwi two points

down. Wilson was excluded when he prematurely put both wheels over the start line in heat seven, and in the re-run Collins won by passing Persson on the second lap.

By now track conditions had become critical, even though it had been watered after heat four. In winning heat eight Michanek covered the crowds on the first-bend terraces in dust, while Jansson, Gordeev and Glucklich chopped and changed positions at the back, Jansson finishing in second place. Heat nine brought together four top names, Michanek, Mauger, Crump, and Collins, but before it was run the track was watered again. Irate fans jumped the fence to assist in the proceedings before the race could get under way. But the watering process had been taken to extremes, and while Michanek passed Mauger down the back straight, Crump and Collins were sprayed in wet shale thrown up by the leaders, and were unable to get on terms. Collins's last place threw English hearts into despair.

Simmons won heat 10 after Jancarz had drifted wide, but when Olsen was out in front in heat 11 Plech fell and the race was halted. Olsen made no mistake in the re-run, however, easily beating Jansson and Persson. Louis revived British enthusiasm when he won heat 12, with Gordeev having little trouble in keeping Wilson in third place, but after all riders had had three outings Olsen was still two points clear of the pack with an unbeaten nine points. Michanek, Louis, Crump and Simmons were bunched on seven points, and Mauger and Collins had six.

Olsen continued his winning form in heat 13, beating Wilson and Crump, and Collins came back on form with victory in the next race. Michanek maintained his challenge by besting Louis in heat 15, but Simmons's chance of a major overall placing disappeared when he finished third. Mauger demonstrated that he was no has-been by taking heat 16 from the forceful Trofimov, and Louis completed his rides in heat 17, winning from Crump and ending with a 12-point total. Michanek won the 18th heat in a canter to ensure himself of runner-up spot at least, but the final outcome of the major placings still depended

Ole Olsen takes the lead in heat 13 from Ray Wilson on the inside, and Phil Crump at the rear.

the series of the start of beat ni.
From left, Peter Collins, Phil Crump, An
Michanek, and Ivan Mauger.
Right: Sweden's Tommy Jansson raises
curtain of the dust that caused so much a
during the 1975 final.
Left: John Louis' spirited riding gained hir
place on the rostrum with 12 points.

on the last two races. Mauger won the 19th heat to enforce a run-off, but what that race would decide still waited on Olsen's performance in heat 20. If the Dane won or was placed second he would be champion, if he finished third he would enter a run-off with Michanek for the title, but if he was last, dropped out with machine problems, or fell he would have to compete with Mauger and Louis in a run-off for second and third positions. As it happened there was little drama — Olsen won the race as he pleased to lift the world championship from 1974 winner Michanek, while Simmons and Collins provided entertainment for the crowd by duelling for second place.

The run-off for third place overall offered perhaps the biggest surprise of a very hectic evening, when Louis gated first and fended off Mauger's challenges, which were made more difficult by the state of the track. Louis's proud third place made him the first Englishman to get into the top three in a world final since 1962.

Score Chart

								Total
1	Ole Olsen	Denmark	3	3	3	3	3	15
2	Anders Michanek	Sweden	1	3	3	3	3	13
3	John Louis	England	2	2	3	2	3	12
4	Ivan Mauger	New Zealand	3	1	2	3	3	12
5	Peter Collins	England	3	3	0	3	1	10
	Phil Crump	Australia	3	3	1	1	2	10
	Malcolm Simmons	England	2	2	3	1	2	10
8	Viktor Trofimov	USSR	2	1	2	2	1	8
9	Tommy Jansson	Sweden	1	2	2	2	f	7
10	Bernt Persson	Sweden	0	2	1	0	2	5
	Ray Wilson	England	0	exc	1	2	2	5
12	Edward Jancarz	Poland	2	0	1	1	0	4
	Valeri Gordeev	USSR	1	1	2	0	0	4
	Zenon Plech	Poland	1	1	f	1	1	4
15	Marek Cieslak	Poland	0	0	0	0	1	1
16	Henryk Glucklich	Poland	0	0	0	0	0	0
	Vladimir Gordeev (res)	USSR	0					0
	Martin Ashby (res)	England	(did not ride)					

Heat-by-heat

		Time
1	Crump, Jancarz, Valeri Gordeev, Persson	73.0s
2	Mauger, Simmons, Jansson, Wilson	71.0s
3	Collins, Louis, Plech, Glucklich	71.2s
4	Olsen, Trofimov, Michanek, Cieslak	71.2s
5	Crump, Simmons, Plech, Cieslak	71.6s
6	Olsen, Louis, Mauger, Jancarz	70.4s
7	Collins, Persson, Trofimov, Vladimir Gordeev, Wilson (exc)	71.6s
8	Michanek, Jansson, Valeri Gordeev, Glucklich	71.6s
9	Michanek, Mauger, Crump, Collins	71.2s
10	Simmons, Trofimov, Jancarz, Glucklich	70.6s
11	Olsen, Jansson, Persson, Plech (exc)	70.8s
12	Louis, Valeri Gordeev, Wilson, Cieslak	71.0s
13	Olsen, Wilson, Crump, Glucklich	71.4s
14	Collins, Jansson, Jancarz, Cieslak	71.2s
15	Michanek, Louis, Simmons, Persson	70.6s
16	Mauger, Trofimov, Plech, Valeri Gordeev	70.4s
17	Louis, Crump, Trofimov, Jansson (f)	70.6s
18	Michanek, Wilson, Plech, Jancarz	70.6s
19	Mauger, Persson, Cieslak, Glucklich	71.4s
20	Olsen, Simmons, Collins, Valeri Gordeev	69.8s
21	Louis beat Mauger in run-off for 3rd place.	69.6s

1976
England's glory revived

AFTER THE USUAL series of qualifying rounds, finals and grand finals had been raced, Sweden backed out of the 1976 world championship without having a rider in the world final proper for the first time in 25 years. Anders Michanek was reserve for the event at Katowice in Poland, but not since 1951 had there been a world final without a Swedish rider competing in the main programme. In contrast, America was represented for the first time in a quarter of a century by Scott Autrey.

The largest ever speedway audience, 120,000, packed the Slaski stadium for what promised to be a great meeting between riders representing eight nations. Egon Muller, the exciting West German, set the ball rolling by breaking the track record in the first heat, winning from Autrey and home riders Jerzy Rembas and Marek Cieslak. In heat two Ivan Mauger gained revenge for his defeat at the hands of John Louis in the previous year's run-off for third place by leading the Englishman home, with Edward Jancarz and Valeri Gordeev at the back.

Heat three saw tremendous action from Peter Collins, who came from the back to lower the track record further and beat Jiri Stancl, Zenon Plech and Doug Wyer. Phil Crump led home Malcolm Simmons, Chris Morton and the other Gordeev brother, Vladimir, in heat four, and then went out again in the next race to score a really lucky win. Mauger was leading easily when he pulled out with a freak mechanical problem — the carburettor slide block broke on his works Jawa. Muller's hopes also faded as he took third place in this race behind Plech.

Heat six saw a more confident Wyer lead from the gate to beat Autrey and Jancarz, and then in heat seven the crowds were able to see Collins at his fighting best. Left at the gate, he took two laps to overhaul Louis and another one-and-a-half to pass Simmons. In doing so he lowered the race record for the 384-metre track yet again, leaving it at 72.2 seconds — it had stood at 74.0 seconds before the meeting.

In the eighth race Cieslak and Stancl gave Chris Morton and Valeri Gordeev a lesson in speedway riding, but not even rain that started prior to the ninth heat could dampen Collins's ardour — he beat Muller, Morton and Jancarz from the gate and led all the way. The 10th heat saw Simmons dispose of Mauger, who was riding his spare bike, and Autrey and Stancl filled

Heading for the first English 1-2 since 1949, Peter Collins (right) and Malcolm Simmons blaze round the Slaski stadium.

Inset: Left to right: Simmons, Collins, and Phil Crump on the rostrum.

Score Chart

								Total
1 Peter Collins	England	3	3	3	3	2		14
2 Malcolm Simmons	England	2	2	3	3	3		13
3 Phil Crump	Australia	3	3	2	1	3		12
4 Ivan Mauger	New Zealand	3	ef	2	3	3		11
Zenon Plech	Poland	1	2	3	2	3		11
6 John Louis	England	2	1	1	3	2		9
7 Doug Wyer	England	0	3	3	1	1		8
Egon Muller	West Germany	3	1	2	2	f		8
9 Scott Autrey	USA	2	2	1	2	0		7
10 Jiri Stancl	Czechoslovakia	2	2	0	1	1		6
Chris Morton	England	1	1	1	2	1		6
12 Edward Jancarz	Poland	1	1	0	1	2		5
13 Marek Cieslak	Poland	0	3	0	ef	1		4
14 Jerzy Rembas	Poland	1	0	2	0	0		3
15 Valeri Gordeev	USSR	0	0	1	0	exc		1
16 Vladimir Gordeev	USSR	0	0	0	0	0		0
Anders Michanek (res)	Sweden					2		2
Grigori Chlynovski (res)	USSR	(did not ride)						

Heat-by-heat

		Time
1	Muller, Autrey, Rembas, Cieslak	72.6s
2	Mauger, Louis, Jancarz, Valeri Gordeev	73.1s
3	Collins, Stancl, Plech, Wyer	72.5s
4	Crump, Simmons, Morton, Vladimir Gordeev	73.7s
5	Crump, Plech, Muller, Mauger (ef)	73.7s
6	Wyer, Autrey, Jancarz, Vladimir Gordeev	73.5s
7	Collins, Simmons, Louis, Rembas	72.2s
8	Cieslak, Stancl, Morton, Valeri Gordeev	74.0s
9	Collins, Muller, Morton, Jancarz	72.4s
10	Simmons, Mauger, Autrey, Stancl	72.9s
11	Plech, Rembas, Valeri Gordeev, Vladimir Gordeev	74.1s
12	Wyer, Crump, Louis, Cieslak	74.0s
13	Louis, Muller, Stancl, Vladimir Gordeev	72.8s
14	Collins, Autrey, Crump, Valeri Gordeev	72.4s
15	Mauger, Morton, Wyer, Rembas	73.2s
16	Simmons, Plech, Jancarz, Cieslak (ef)	73.0s
17	Simmons, Michanek, Wyer, Muller (f), Valeri Gordeev (exc)	74.0s
18	Plech, Louis, Morton, Autrey (f)	72.8s
19	Crump, Jancarz, Stancl, Rembas	74.4s
20	Mauger, Collins, Cieslak, Vladimir Gordeev	73.4s

the minor placings. Plech won the next race, in which the two Gordeevs were left at the back, and in heat 12 Wyer beat the determined Crump, while John Louis was a disappointing third. With all contestants now having had three rides, Collins was the only unbeaten man, Crump lurked closely on eight points, Simmons had seven, and Plech, Wyer and Muller were on six.

Muller gated first in heat 13, but Louis had other ideas about the outcome of the race and beat the West German on the run-in to the flag, with Stancl in third place. Collins came out for his fourth ride in heat 14, and won it from the gate while Crump dropped a vital point to Autrey. After the disappointments in his two previous rides, Mauger returned to form in the 15th heat, beating Wyer from the gate. Morton then came up to grab second place.

Simmons had three Poles to contend with in heat 16, but made a rapid exit from the gate and won comfortably from Plech, Jancarz and Cieslak. Understandably, the crowd was none too pleased with the performance of the trio in this race. Muller had a chance to get on to the rostrum in heat 17, and looked as though he was going to make it when he led the restart after Valeri Gordeev had been excluded for breaking the tapes. But after holding on for two laps he overdid things and crashed over the handlebars, leaving Simmons to win from reserve Michanek and Wyer. This result gave Simmons a total of 13 points, enough to guarantee him a placing among the top three. The Polish fans warmed to a fine win by Plech in heat 18, when he outpaced Louis with Morton taking a point for third place after Autrey had fallen. Crump needed to win heat 19 to get among the top three, and he succeeded in doing so with victory over Jancarz and Stancl.

The final race was also the decisive one in setting the destination of the world title. It featured Mauger, Cieslak, Vladimir Gordeev and Collins, who needed two points to capture overall victory. Mauger gated first and Collins tucked in behind him to settle for a cool second place — and the world championship. It must have been alien to his natural style to hold back and not attempt to win the title with an unbeaten score, but the 22-year-old used plenty of sense in this race. He was England's first world champion since his childhood hero Peter Craven had taken the title back in 1962. Underlining the new talent that English speedway was now displaying, Simmons took the runner-up position. And to crown a total British monopoly, both the Englishmen were riding machines with the four-valve Weslake engines, the first time that this factory had deposed Jawa from the No 1 position.

Australia, a country that had previously supplied four world champions, was represented in third place by Crump. But of the Poles, who had been successful when they last staged the world final in 1973, their best rider was Plech, in joint fourth place.

Doug Wyer, pictured leading Phil Crump, stormed to an eight-point total in his world final debut.

1977 Mr Cool makes it five

Finn Thomsen becomes the only rider to defeat Ivan Mauger (left) in the 1977 final. Billy Sanders is in the background. Thomsen's 10 points made him fifth overall.

IN LINE with speedway's ever-growing international appeal, the most complex series of eliminating rounds yet devised was arranged to sort out the 16 qualifiers for the 1977 final, which returned to Gothenburg in Sweden. This season there was an American and Australasian preliminary, in addition to the traditional knock-out tournaments staged in Britain and on the Continent. These meetings led up to a Continental final at White City in London and a Swedish final to decide the world final entrants. To many enthusiasts all this seemed a most unsatisfactory way of running things, and led to suggestions that a more practical method would be needed in future seasons.

The final itself suffered from both the weather and from injuries to Peter Collins and Anders Michanek, both of the former world champions having crashed only a matter of days before the big event. Collins incurred a broken left leg and needed 32 stitches in a gash in the limb, and left hospital only the day before the final. He hobbled to his bike for each of his rides, and needed crutches to get about in the pits. Michanek was suffering from a broken right foot, and between races had to prop his leg on a chair in the pits.

A steady drizzle and a late start hardly seemed like good omens for the racing, but Egon Muller startled the 35,000 crowd by winning the first heat in a fast time, with Finn Thomsen and John Boulger looking in good form behind him. Michanek and Ivan Mauger lined up to do battle in heat two, but the New Zealander got away first while Michanek accepted second place after first unsettling Edward Jancarz.

Ole Olsen made an unfortunate start to the evening when he was brought under the two-minute rule for being late out of the pits. He made it to the line within the time allowance, but then missed the gate and was unable to catch Australian Billy Sanders who won his debut ride in a world final. Bernt Persson and Jan Mucha were never in contention in this race.

Collins overcame the handicap of his injury to beat teenager Michael Lee and Bengt Jansson in heat four. In the next race Olsen again came under the two-minute rule and again missed the gate after reaching the start area on time. Muller pulled out in front, but Olsen recovered his temperament to snatch victory on the last bend, while Michanek retired from the race, knowing that he had no chance of breaking the wall of damp shale thrown up by the leaders.

Collins pulled off another win in heat six, leading from the gate and comfortably beating Boulger. Mauger made a poor start in heat seven, while in front of him Sanders and Thomsen tangled on the first turn. Mauger passed Sanders, but was unable to catch the young Dane. Lee proved his potential in heat eight by coming from the back after a scuffle on the first turn to defeat Swedes Tommy Nilsson and Persson. Then Lee promptly went out again in the next race, this time to beat Sanders after some hair-raising riding on the first turn.

The drizzle turned to rain for the 10th heat, but it didn't trouble Michanek, who won from Persson, while Boulger was unlucky enough to suffer engine trouble after making a good start. Incredibly, Olsen came under the two-minute warning for the third occasion prior to heat 11, but once again he rolled up to the tapes in time. Collins got out of the gate first, but Olsen was too good for the handicapped world champion and took the lead, as his opponent rode the last two laps in agony.

By now the rain had made the track surface difficult, and the racing was suffering in consequence. But Mauger was not deterred from winning heat 12 from a determined Jansson. Heat 13 was re-run after Muller had fallen on the first turn in the original start. Again Mauger made no mistake to lead Collins all the way and become favourite to end the night as world champion.

Boulger led heat 14 briefly, being passed by Jansson, and heat 15 resulted in a win for Michanek after Thomsen had disputed Lee's position on the starting grid. Unaffected by nerves, Lee promptly beat Thomsen into third place. Olsen drew the inevitable two-minute warning in heat 16, only to win as he pleased once he appeared. Heat 17 saw a win by Muller and two exclusions — Jan Verner for illegal tactics at the start and Mucha for being lapped — but now the crowd was eager for heat 18, which would bring together Olsen, Mauger and Lee.

Olsen and Mauger were level on points at this stage, and Lee was only one point behind them — it was clearly going to be a crucial race. A ragged start resulted in a re-run being ordered, and at the second attempt Boulger surprised everyone by taking the lead. However, his riding tactics were hardly suited to the tricky conditions, and he crashed, an action that resulted in Olsen laying down his machine to avoid the

fallen rider and damaging it in the process. Boulger was excluded from the second re-run, and after much delay, the mighty Mauger rode faultlessly to lead from the gate, with Lee holding second place. Riding a borrowed machine, Olsen was never in contention for anything other than third place.

In the run-off to decide third place overall behind Mauger and Collins, Olsen beat Lee in atrocious conditions. Some critics suggested that Mauger had had more than his share of luck in winning on this particular night, but it was really his cool temperament and vast experience that helped him to equal Ove Fundin's record of five world championships.

Picture captures the elation of Ivan Mauger after he had won his last ride to clinch the title in rain-soaked conditions. His total of five championships equalled the record set by Sweden's Ove Fundin.

The tapes fly up on (from left) John Boulger, Jiri Stancl, Anders Michanek, and Bernt Persson. Michanek was the most successful of the quartet, scoring eight points despite two retirements.

Score Chart

									Total
1	Ivan Mauger	New Zealand	3	2	3	3	3	14
2	Peter Collins	England	3	3	2	2	3	13
3	Ole Olsen	Denmark	2	3	3	3	1	12
4	Michael Lee	England	2	3	3	2	2	12
5	Finn Thomsen	Denmark	2	3	1	1	3	10
6	Bengt Jansson	Sweden	1	1	2	3	2	9
7	Egon Muller	W Germany	3	2	0	f/e	3	8
	Anders Michanek	Sweden	2	ret	3	3	ret	8
9	Tommy Nilsson	Sweden	0	2	ret	2	2	6
	Billy Sanders	Australia	3	1	2	0	ret	6
	Bernt Persson	Sweden	1	1	2	1	1	6
12	John Boulger	Australia	1	2	ef	2	f/e	5
13	Edward Jancarz	Poland	1	1	1	1	0	4
14	Jiri Stancl	Czechoslovakia	0	0	1	0	2	3
15	Jan Verner	Czechoslovakia	0	0	0	1	exc	1
	Jan Mucha	Poland	0	0	1	ret	exc	1
	John Davis (res)	England	(did not ride)					
	Soren Karlsson (res)	Sweden	(did not ride)					
	Boguslaw Nowak (res)	Poland	(did not ride)					

Heat-by-heat

		Time
1	Muller, Thomsen, Boulger, Nilsson	74.6s
2	Mauger, Michanek, Jancarz, Verner	76.1s
3	Sanders, Olsen, Persson, Mucha	76.6s
4	Collins, Lee, Jansson, Stancl	76.7s
5	Olsen, Muller, Jansson, Michanek (ret)	75.6s
6	Collins, Boulger, Jancarz, Mucha	77.7s
7	Thomsen, Mauger, Sanders, Stancl	77.6s
8	Lee, Nilsson, Persson, Verner	77.7s
9	Lee, Sanders, Jancarz, Muller	76.1s
10	Michanek, Persson, Stancl, Boulger (ef)	79.2s
11	Olsen, Collins, Thomsen, Verner	75.5s
12	Mauger, Jansson, Mucha, Nilsson (ret)	78.0s
13	Mauger, Collins, Persson, Muller (f/exc)	75.9s
14	Jansson, Boulger, Verner, Sanders	76.9s
15	Michanek, Lee, Thomsen, Mucha (ret)	77.6s
16	Olsen, Nilsson, Jancarz, Stancl	77.9s
17	Muller, Stancl, Mucha (exc), Verner (exc)	79.5s
18	Mauger, Lee, Olsen, Boulger (exc)	79.5s
19	Thomsen, Jansson, Persson, Jancarz (ret)	80.5s
20	Collins, Nilsson, Michanek (ret), Sanders (ret)	83.4s
21	Olsen beat Lee in run-off for 3rd place.	81.6s

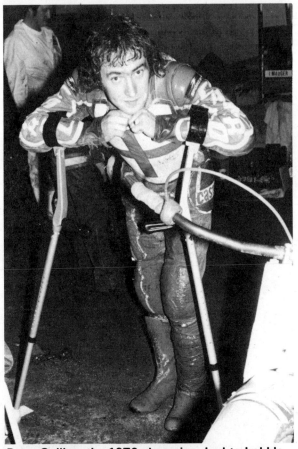

Peter Collins, the 1976 champion, had to hobble around the pits on crutches after suffering a broken leg prior to the 1977 final. He nevertheless finished a bold second overall.

1978
Olsen's golden year

IN THE YEAR that England celebrated the Golden Jubilee of speedway racing's arrival in the country, it was most appropriate that the world final should be held at Wembley stadium. However, before the big night could take place, riders had to engage in the usual long trek through qualifying events throughout the world.

These started in Australasia, and eventually four qualifiers joined the seeded world champion, Ivan Mauger, in the Inter-Continental Final. Of this quartet, only John Titman was able to fight through to Wembley with Mauger, who finished second to Ole Olsen in the Inter-Continental clash after the pair had had to take part in a run-off for the first place. From the Continental Final, which covered riders in West Germany and the East European countries, Hans Wasserman emerged as winner, but was unlucky to suffer an injury prior to Wembley, and his place was taken by Jerzy Rembas.

British qualifying rounds were raced in conjunction with the Volkswagen/*Daily Mirror* Grand Prix event,

Ole Olsen, world champion for the third time.

World final speedway at its closest — from left, Michael Lee, Scott Autrey and Ivan Mauger.

which provoked a certain amount of controversy. From preliminary rounds, the leading 32 scorers contested the semi-finals, and the leading eight men from each of these events went forward to ride in the British Final at Coventry, which was twice postponed because of bad weather. Only four riders were to move forward to Wembley from this tough Coventry meeting, which was tinged with acrimony when Peter Collins, who failed to qualify, alleged that his machines had been sabotaged. But Michael Lee retained his British championship, and was joined at Wembley by Malcolm Simmons, Dave Jessup and Gordon Kennett.

On the day of the final the weather was fine, the track in superb condition, and 90,000 spectators provided a great atmosphere. Heat one saw the American Scott Autrey shatter the track record in beating Simmons, but Lee trimmed the record even further in scoring an easy win in heat two. Rembas, who was to prove a surprise contender for top honours, took advantage of a mechanical failure on early leader Jessup's machine to win heat three, and then the crowd awaited heat four, which was clearly going to be one of the night's crucial races.

In determined mood, Ivan Mauger got away first and looked a likely winner for two laps. However, Olsen and Kennett caught up ground and made the New Zealander the meat in the sandwich as the trio entered the pits turn three abreast. As Olsen and Kennett swept past the reigning champion he appeared to be impeded and fell, knowing that his title had surely slipped away. Olsen took full advantage of the mishap to win from Kennett.

Heat five saw Rembas gate first, but the Pole lost it on the first turn, and Kennett and Simmons stormed on

to take the first two places. As if to prove he was not yet defeated, Mauger beat Autrey in the next race, while Olsen lost out to the fast-gating Anders Michanek in heat seven. Jessup looked good as he beat Titman in the eighth, and then the track record was lowered again when Lee won heat nine from Simmons. The record went for the fourth time when Jessup caused Olsen and Autrey to miss valuable points in heat 10, but an even greater upset occurred in the next race when Rembas passed Mauger from the back and put himself among the leaders. Then Ila Teromaa beat Kennett to leave an interesting situation after all riders had had three outings. Lee, Rembas, Olsen and Kennett were tying on seven points, while only one point behind lay Jessup, Simmons and Autrey.

After the interval, Jessup beat Simmons in heat 13, while Mauger's title hopes finally dived when he finished last. Autrey beat Kennett in heat 14, Titman took the next race to score his only win of the night, and in heat 16 Olsen and Lee put paid to the aspirations of Rembas. Olsen had to appear in the next race, and knew that a good performance would gain him the title. The Dane made no mistake in beating Simmons, and thus inherited the world championship for the third time.

Rembas bounced back to beat Autrey in heat 18, this result placing them both into a run-off for third overall. If either Kennett or Jessup won heat 19, he would fill the runner-up position to Olsen, although it would be a hard race as Lee and Michanek were also on the grid. But Kennett won from Jessup, who must have been thoroughly cursing his ill luck when his bike had stopped in his first outing. That mishap could well have cost him the world title, but at least he was now eligible

In the run-off for third place, Jerzy Rembas pulls a wheelie while Dave Jessup gates smoothly.

Dave Jessup (right) won this battle from Ole Olsen (centre) and Scott Autrey (left).

Finland's first world finalist, IIa Teromaa, holds off England's Gordon Kennett.

to join Rembas and Autrey in the run-off for the final place on the rostrum.

Mauger climaxed his eventful night by winning heat 20 from Teromaa, and then the crowd settled down to await the run-off for third place. But it was not an exciting race, as Rembas threw away his chances by rearing at the gate, and the fast-starting Autrey outrode Jessup. The plucky Autrey thus became the first American to gain a major world final placing since 1938, while Olsen was the fourth rider to win the world title three times, and Kennett became the eighth English rider to take the runner-up position, and was also the third consecutive Englishman to almost win the title in the past three years.

It was a final that had not provided spectacular racing, this factor undoubtedly being due to a closely matched field of top class riders competing on a track in peak condition. However, the lack of passing was made up for by the drama and tension that resulted from all the main contenders dropping points in their early races, and the event proved an appropriate high point to speedway's Golden Jubilee season.

Score Chart

									Total
1	Ole Olsen	Denmark	3	2	2	3	3	13
2	Gordon Kennett	England	2	3	2	2	3	12
3	Scott Autrey	USA	3	2	1	3	2	11
4	Dave Jessup	England	ef	3	3	3	2	11
	Jerzy Rembas	Poland	3	1	3	1	3	11
6	Malcolm Simmons	England	2	2	2	2	2	10
7	Michael Lee	England	3	1	3	2	0	9
8	Ivan Mauger	New Zealand	f	3	2	0	3	8
9	John Titman	Australia	1	2	f	3	1	7
	Anders Michanek	Sweden	1	3	0	2	1	7
11	IIa Teromaa	Finland	0	1	3	f	2	6
12	Marek Cieslak	Poland	2	0	1	1	1	5
	Jan Verner	Czechoslovakia	2	1	1	0	1	5
14	Jan Andersson	Sweden	1	0	1	1	0	3
15	Jiri Stancl	Czechoslovakia	1	0	0	1	0	2
16	Petra Ondrasik	Czechoslovakia	f/r	0	0	0	0	0
	Bernt Persson (res)	Sweden	(did not ride)					
	Zdenek Kudrna (res)	Czechoslovakia	(did not ride)					
	Steve Bastable (res)	England	(did not ride)					

Heat-by-heat

		Time
1	Autrey, Simmons, Michanek, Teromaa	67.4s
2	Lee, Cieslak, Stancl, Ondrasik	67.3s
3	Rembas, Verner, Andersson, Jessup (ef)	68.9s
4	Olsen, Kennett, Titman, Mauger (f)	68.0s
5	Kennett, Simmons, Rembas, Ondrasik (f/re)	67.6s
6	Mauger, Autrey, Lee, Andersson	67.9s
7	Michanek, Olsen, Verner, Stancl	67.7s
8	Jessup, Titman, Teromaa, Cieslak	67.4s
9	Lee, Simmons, Verner, Titman (f)	67.1s
10	Jessup, Olsen, Autrey, Ondrasik	67.0s
11	Rembas, Mauger, Cieslak, Michanek	67.3s
12	Teromaa, Kennett, Andersson, Stancl	67.6s
13	Jessup, Simmons, Stancl, Mauger	67.3s
14	Autrey, Kennett, Cieslak, Verner	67.2s
15	Titman, Michanek, Andersson, Ondrasik	68.7s
16	Olsen, Lee, Rembas, Teromaa (f)	67.2s
17	Olsen, Simmons, Cieslak, Andersson	67.3s
18	Rembas, Autrey, Titman, Stancl (f)	67.2s
19	Kennett, Jessup, Michanek, Lee	67.6s
20	Mauger, Teromaa, Verner, Ondrasik	67.8s
21	Autrey beat Jessup and Rembas in run-off for 3rd place.	67.6s

The pioneer years by Mike Nicks

THOSE WERE the days . . . in the rip-roaring 1930s when a top rider could earn the price of a house in a week's racing, and in speedway's post-war boom when the sport's champions were feted like national heroes. Today's world finals offer a spectacle of speed, colour and professionalism unmatched by any other era, but the championship's early times had something of a wild, barn-storming charm that has long since disappeared.

Jack Parker, for example, literally did win the price of a house in a week of racing during the period when the pre-war *Star* championships were evolving into what were to become the world finals. One of a large family, Jack wanted to buy his mother a smaller, more manageable home once the youngsters had moved out to find their own ways in the world. She went on holiday, and returned to find that Jack had purchased and furnished a new home for her. 'I earned the money to do that in just one week, and recently I was offered £20,000 for that house. Can a world speedway champion earn £20,000 a week these days? They're just racing for tram tickets now,' he affirms.

Jack never won a world final, but he took the *Star* Championship in 1934 and the British Riders' title in 1947, and is generally revered as one of speedway's all-time greats. He recalls those crazy early days with vivid clarity. He was earning £2.80 a week as an engineer for the BSA motorcycle factory when the company sent him to investigate the strange new sport of dirt track racing that was sweeping Britain in the late twenties. 'I took a standard road bike to the High Beech track and won a handicap race and was second in the scratch race final. The following Monday the Wimbledon track was due to open, and the promoter asked me to ride in a match race with Vic Huxley, who was the top rider at that time. They offered me £50 if I could win, and £25 if I lost. That was at a time when the works manager at BSA was only getting £1,000 a year.

'Well, I went along to Wimbledon, but I couldn't get anywhere near Huxley's dirt track Douglas on my road bike. But I returned to the BSA factory in Birmingham, spent 10 days building a special bike, and then returned to London to go speedway racing.'

Jack's victory in the 1934 *Star* Championship was

Two of speedway's all-time greats, Jack Parker (left) and Vic Duggan, during a pre-war confrontation at Wembley.

achieved at the expense of Eric Langton, who he admired as one of the sport's most under-rated riders. 'His results record may not look that good, but he was brilliant as a rider and an engineer. He could also lick me out of the gate every time, and I won that 1934 championship by passing him on the pits turn at Wembley.'

Typical of the zany happenings of the period, Jack was expected to take part in a swimming race at the opening of Wembley's Empire Pool that coincided with the dinner to celebrate his victory. Leading competitors in various sports had been invited to enter the race, but Jack won it — and found a cheque for £25 by his plate when he had changed and returned to the dinner table.

Jack remembers that the atmosphere surrounding the first world final in 1936 was fantastic. 'It was a terrific event from every point of view, and this was because Sir Arthur Elvin, who ran Wembley, had flair and was a perfectionist. His show had to be flawless or someone would get the sack. Nothing else mattered but the presentation — not even the riders.'

Prior to the 1936 event Jack had won 36 consecutive races, but shortly before the world final he had looped his bike at the start of a race on the West Ham track, and broken a wrist. Thus he was unable to ride in the meeting, but he was back in action for the 1937 final, when the American trio of Jack Milne, Wilbur Lamoreaux, and Cordy Milne performed their famous feat of finishing first, second and third. Jack was fourth, two points behind Cordy.

'Jack Milne had a tremendous advantage that year,' he says. 'He was riding for the New Cross team, and their promoter was getting exclusive supplies of a special tyre called the "Leap Ahead". It gave better grip and it was certainly one of the reasons why Jack was unbeaten that night.'

During his career Jack was at the centre of several of speedway's innovations, including the mass switch

from the spectacular leg-trailing style to the modern foot-forward method. 'I was a leg-trailer at first, because when you're new to something and you see people performing it in a certain way, you tend to imitate them. But I soon began to look carefully at riding styles, and I realised that there were disadvantages to leg-trailing. For example, it tended to make a rider go wide on the corners. Oliver Hart was a great leg-trailer, but over a four-lap race he would travel perhaps 60 or 70 yards further than me. So once I had changed to the foot-forward style, I would keep to the inside and always beat him.'

Jack recalls that the foot-forward revolution was pioneered by the Wembley league team. They realised that by keeping the left foot out and forward a rival rider could be prevented from overtaking on the inside. Once he had adopted the new style, Jack, always a

Two dramatic shots that explain speedway's boom in Britain's bleak post-war years. Below, Split Waterman leads Jack Parker in a furious duel; right, the same pair, again with Waterman in front, get into impossible situations during a later clash in the 1951 season, a year when both finished among the top five in the world final.

rider who used his brain as well as his skill and courage, added his personal modification. 'I had my front wheel painted yellow, and everyone thought it was because yellow was part of the Harringay colours, the team I was riding for at that time. What they didn't know was that the yellow wheel acted as a secret signal between me and Bill Pitcher, who was my riding partner in the team. If he saw a yellow front wheel creeping up on his inside, he would move out slightly so that between us we could block the track and stop anyone else from getting by.'

Jack Parker is remembered more for his legendary ability to win two-man match-races rather than for his performance in world finals, an event he openly refers to as 'a lottery'. He explains: 'Finding a champion from 16 riders in just one night's racing is like throwing someone into a swimming pool packed with piranhas and telling them that they can win if they get to the other side without being bitten. Having four riders in a race makes everything too unpredictable. That's why I never went into a final with the intention of cleaning up. I just went along to ride as well as I could. I could never get my mind perfectly clear unless I was involved in match racing with just one other rider on the track.

'That's why I won the British Riders Championship in 1947 — because Bill Kitchen and I had to take part in a decider after we had both scored 14 points. Bill was a good rider and had the most intense desire to get to the top that I've ever encountered. But he never really knew what shape the Wembley track was. He did his best, but it's a difficult track to ride, and he used to drift too wide on the exit from the last corner. I passed him on that last corner on the last lap because he was still sliding outwards at the point when he should have

107

been straightening up and getting drive towards the finish line.'

Tommy Price, winner of the first post-war world final in 1949 and the first English world champion, was also a rider who paid a lot of respect to the challenging demands of the Wembley track. Its problem is that its bends run over the corners of the stadium's famous soccer pitch, preventing the turns from being banked, as they are on many speedway tracks. This means that it is difficult for riders to pass on the outside, and gaining grip on the exit from the turns is a delicate and crucial business.

'If you ride at Wembley and are feeling tired from meetings earlier in the week, you could well perform better than a man who arrives fit and full of beans, because his exuberance could prove a handicap,' Tommy believes. 'I've stood on the centre green at Wembley and watched a particular rider put on a brilliant show, and I've anticipated a hard race with him. But when we've met in a heat I've tootled around the bends close to the white line and finished the race a second faster than the more spectacular man.'

Tommy, who also won the 1946 British Riders Championship, had another advantage when he was racing at Wembley, for he was never affected by the notorious 'big night nerves' that have been the downfall of so many potential champions in world final competition. 'Quite the opposite — the atmosphere of a world final night actually made me a better man,' he recalls. What is it like to perform in the famous Wembley arena in front of almost 100,000 roaring fans? 'Behind the track lights everything fades into blackness, so it's like being on the stage. You can't see the crowd or hear them — at least, I never heard them, but I suppose it depends on how hard you concentrate on your racing. All you are aware of is the track and the safety fence — people are the last thing you ever know about.'

Posing in a speedway sweater for *Pins and Needles* **knitting magazine was just one of Tommy Price's**

Tommy's 1949 world title was gained the hard way. He had started the season in poor style, and Sir Arthur Elvin's Wembley management, for whom he rode in league racing, had decided in typically dictatorial fashion that he would have to qualify for the final by first competing in an eliminating round on a Second Division track. This both irritated and worried Tommy, particularly as he was drawn to ride on the Newcastle track, an oval he had not previously seen. On arrival at the track, he examined its unusual shape made up of long straights and tight corners, and felt even more uneasy at the presence of Arthur Forrest, the so-called 'Black Prince' who was the top Second Division rider at the time. But Tommy went out to complete five unbeaten rides and set the fastest time of the night. Later, as his form continued to improve, he dominated the qualifying rounds on First Division tracks in company with Australia's 'blond bombshell', Graham Warren.

One handicap he had to fight off was his annual attack of hay fever, which would often lead him to spend sunny days fettling his bikes in the shelter of the workshops at the Wembley track, while the rest of the population headed for the open air and the countryside. But in the weeks leading up to the 1949 final he was mentally gearing himself to win.

As it happened, on the night of the final he won all his races from the gate, except for one dramatic heat when Wilbur Lamoreaux hit the first bend in the lead. Tommy remembers the race and its aftermath well:

'"Lammy" was very light, and so he often used to get out of the gate first, as he did in this race. I tried to pass him, but my bike hit a bump which threw the front wheel into the air. By the time I had sorted that out I'd dropped to third place behind Ron Clarke, and I had to set about catching the leaders. I got up on the inside of Lammy, right behind him with Ron Clarke outside me. Then I heard Lammy's motor cough and I just zoomed

engagements during his years at the top. Above: Vic Duggan leads Dent Oliver in a 1949 race.

through on the inside and won the race.

'Some writers in the press said that I was lucky to win the championship because of Lammy's engine trouble, but I disagreed. The JAP engines had been giving this particular trouble all season, and Lammy had been experiencing it for two or three weeks before the final. What was happening was that oil was building up in the cam box of the engines and fouling the sparking plug when it seeped into the cylinder head. I'd cured the problem on my bikes, so there was no reason why other riders couldn't have done the same.'

At this time the world final was still being raced on a Thursday night, and the next evening Tommy was booked to ride at Harringay, where he would have to meet the great Vic Duggan. Injury had prevented Duggan from qualifying for the world final, but Tommy sensed that if he was defeated at Harringay, the press would hail Duggan as the true champion in all but name. So, with the dedication that was a hallmark of his career, Tommy elected to miss the traditional post-final dinner and dance, and headed for home and sleep. The mighty Sir Arthur Elvin even sent a chauffeur and a car to Tommy's home in an attempt to wheedle him to the festivities, but he declined — and the next night he duly defeated Duggan on the Harringay oval.

At the peak of his career Tommy regularly earned between £250 and £350 a week — equivalent to about £1,500 at today's prices — and after each of his 1946 and 1949 Wembley victories he joined the ranks of the famous at Madame Tussaud's renowned wax-works in London. He was acclaimed as a national hero, and appeared in advertisements for Quaker Oats, Y-front underwear, and the Cord piston ring company.

Tommy always prepared his own bikes, as he considered the official Wembley team mechanics did not work to his high standards. With his two bikes and half-dozen spare engines, he was always experimenting and producing little tricks that kept his machines that vital bit faster than most of the opposition's. Along with the JAP company and other leading riders, he was at the forefront of technical developments that pared the weight of his championship machines from 250lb in 1946 to 180lb only three years later.

But, ironically, it was a mechanical fault that cost him the chance of retaining his world championship in 1950. He built a special machine for the event, with a frame formed from chrome-molybdenum steel tubing by the well known speedway engineer, Mike Erskine. If this material has to be heated for any reason, it must be 'normalised' afterwards at a certain temperature in a furnace if it is to retain its strength. The week before the 1950 final Tommy suffered a crash which bent the chrome-molybdenum frame, but after heating and straightening the chassis he had no time to normalise it. In the final he won his first race easily, beating Aub Lawson. In his second race he was riding neck-and-neck with Dent Oliver, but holding the advantageous inside position, when he mysteriously crashed. Uninjured, he discovered that the frame had bent

again, and realised that his failure to give it the strengthening treatment in an oven had cost him the chance of defending his title.

The man who inherited the crown experienced a mercurial path to fame that typified the sensational happenings during speedway's boom in the early fifties. In a series of episodes that would be regarded as unbelievable if they were used as the basis of a boys' comic story, Freddie Williams rose from the obscurity of an apprentice fitter at Portsmouth naval dockyard to win the World Speedway Championship twice, all in the space of six years.

The improbable Williams tale began in Wales, where he enjoyed a few outings in grass track races on his father's 500cc Matchless. Then, while he was working in Portsmouth after the war, the management of the illustrious Wembley league team embarked on a process of building up an all-British team. Advertisements were placed in the motorcycling press requesting young hopefuls to apply for places at trial riding sessions. The youthful Williams had not even seen a speedway race, let alone handled a speedway bike, yet he wrote off, carefully disguising his total lack of experience.

Freddie was one of some 300 applicants who were asked to ride in the trials, and was told to arrive at Wembley stadium at eight o'clock one morning. Like a latter-day Dick Whittington, he disembarked from the train the previous night, and walked the streets of the great capital wondering where he could stay. He sought advice from a policeman, who suggested the hour was too late for locating a room, and offered the comfort of a cell in the police station for the night. Woken the next morning with a cup of tea and a bun for breakfast, the future world champion was then guided onto the tube train for Wembley!

Together with about 20 other young hopefuls, he was then bundled into the back of a Bedford van, and delivered to the Rye House training track in Hertfordshire, where they sorted out racing equipment from a large box of leathers, helmets and boots.

'They had half a dozen speedway bikes there. First we had to ride round the track a couple of times individually, then they started organising us into four-man races,' Freddie recollects. The Wembley league riders supervising the tests must have been reasonably impressed with his potential, for a couple of weeks later he received a postcard summoning him for a further session. He eventually attended five or six of these training sessions before all the contenders had been whittled down to a hard-core of a dozen riders who were judged to have real ability. 'Those trials were real blood-baths — everyone was falling off and crashing,' Freddie laughs.

For his first full season with Wembley in 1948, he was supplied with a bike by the team, the cost of which was deducted in instalments from his weekly earnings. He qualified for his first world final in 1950, and was certainly not regarded as one of the favourites. But Freddie and his mechanic, Cyril Spinks, devised a tactic that was intended to shatter the morale of the other riders. 'I was due to ride in the first

Left: Jack Young: 'He cornered so hard it was a wonder the handlebars didn't break.' Right: Vic Duggan takes a breather in the pits.

race of the night, and we knew that if I could break the track record in that heat it would be a devastating blow to everyone else.'

And that's exactly what Freddie managed, trimming the record for the 344-metre Wembley oval to exactly 71 seconds as he led home Wally Green, Ron Clarke and Jack Biggs. His only defeat of the night occurred in heat 14, when Aub Lawson gated first, but the wily Jack Parker slipped into the lead and was able to hold Freddie back in second place.

In the 1951 final Freddie was joined by his brother Eric, but both suffered a mediocre meeting, scoring seven and six points respectively. In 1952, however, Freddie made a return to form, and at Wembley he repeated his 1950 tactic by winning the first race of the night in a devastating time of 69.6 seconds — the first sub-70-second race in world final history. But Freddie reckoned without the inspired aggression of the fantastic Jack Young. The Australian had created a sensation the previous season by winning the world championship while still a Second Division rider. Jack Parker paid this tribute to the riding ability of the man with the looks of a Hollywood movie star: 'I thought I could throw a bike into a turn faster than anyone until I saw Jack Young. He was all shoulders, and when he forced the bike into a corner it was a wonder the handlebars didn't break.'

The 1952 clash between Williams and Young was scheduled for heat six, and it developed into a race that the Welshman still regrets. 'I should have won it,' he reflects, 'but I completely misread what "Youngie" would do. I made the gate on him, but he was like a tiger behind me and just wouldn't give up. I'm sure that on one bend he had his front wheel on the grass while trying to pass me on the inside. For three laps I led him, but on every corner I could hear his engine just behind me. Then I heard him moving up outside me going down the back straight, so I went wide into the next corner and threw my back wheel at him. I heard the clanging and scraping of his bike hitting the fence behind me. and at that point I thought I'd got rid of him by putting him through the fence. So no one was more

surprised than me when he came inside me on the next turn.'

The Australian swept on to become the first man to win two world finals, while Freddie Williams had to be content with runner-up position. But his frank admission of his attempt to send Young crashing through the safety fence acts as a vivid reminder of the world final fever that can grip riders.

Freddie was able to gain revenge in 1953, when he again used his planned approach to the final. He worked out the strategy he would use against particular riders, and made a great start by winning the opening race in what was to be the fastest time of the night. Geoff Mardon was the rider he feared most, but when the pair met in heat 13 it was Jeff Lloyd who won, with Williams holding Mardon back in third place.

After all riders had had four outings Split Waterman remained unbeaten, while Williams had dropped one point. The pair met in heat 17, and Williams knew he had to keep ahead of Waterman to enforce a run-off for the title. Alternatively, if either Sweden's Olle Nygren or the Australian Aub Lawson relegated Waterman to third or last place, the title would go to Williams without the necessity for a deciding race.

Of the crucial heat 17, Freddie remembers: 'I led all the way from the gate, but coming up the last straight I didn't know whether Waterman had finished second. Then Nygren, a rider I got along with well, pulled alongside me as we turned into the pits and thumped me on the back. He said, "I fix Split for you, Fred." He meant that he had kept Waterman back in third place, and they were the sweetest words I'd ever heard, because I had the feeling that Waterman would have beaten me in a run-off for the title.'

In the following year, a young New Zealander named Ronnie Moore won the final and ushered in a new era of great champions — among them Peter Craven, Ove Fundin, Barry Briggs, Ivan Mauger, and Ole Olsen. But it was the stirring performances of those champions from the thirties, forties and early fifties that established speedway's world final as one of the greatest of international sporting events.

World Final

PhotoFile

Past times: who would have forecast that the 17-year-old Ivan Mauger, pictured (below right) receiving advice from Ron How, would progress to win five world finals? Another enterprising New Zealander, Barry Briggs, had already made it to the top by the time he was photographed (left) with his wife June in the London record shop they owned in the late fifties. What the well-dressed speedway rider of the thirties wore off the track (below left): pre-war finalists Bill Kitchen (left) and Bob Harrison (right) chat with the quaintly named 'Acorn' Dobson, who never made it to a Wembley final.

Opposite page, top: No wonder speedway was such a crowd-pulling spectacle before the war! From left, Dicky Smythe, Vic Huxley, Jack Parker, and Eric Langton battle for points at Wembley. Below: the incredible 'Sprouts' Elder, who competed in the first *Star* championship in 1929, is reputed to have commanded a £500 appearance fee in speedway's early days.

PhotoFile

Above: the surprise rider who could have won the 1978 world final but for an engine failure, Dave Jessup.
Left: A proud Gordon Kennett on the rostrum after gaining second place in the 1978 final.
Below: England's fighting Peter Collins pours on the power during the 1977 Inter-Continental final.
Opposite page: speedway's king of the 1970s, the brilliant Ole Olsen.

World final action at its finest: John Louis (white helmet) and Zenon Plech fight for the lead, with Chris Morton on the outside and Scott Autrey at the rear, during the 1976 world final in Poland.

Above: only inches separate Anders Michanek (red helmet) and Scott Autrey at the 1976 Inter-Continental round at Wembley. Below left: a Pole and a Swede who have contributed many world final highlights, Edward Jancarz (leading) and Bernt Persson. Below right: Sweden 1974 – Zenon Plech (11) and Peter Collins lead Tommy Johansson (7) and Tommy Jansson.

Ivan Mauger'sfinal solution

Victorious again! Ivan Mauger poses with actress Alexandra Bastedo, runner-up Bernt Persson (left) and third placed Ole Olsen at Wembley in 1972.

by Peter Oakes

CALL Ivan Mauger during world final week and the odds are the phone will ring and ring. Unless you know a special code, the New Zealander's private phone will be left unanswered, for the days before a world final see him withdraw into a shell.

Nothing is more important than the meeting ahead. Casual acquaintances who happen to meet Mauger and his former schoolgirl sweetheart Raye during the approach to the really big fixture of the season must wonder if the couple's marriage is on the rocks. The five-times world champion, who was awarded the MBE for his services to speedway, is likely to bark at Raye incessantly. He is moody. He is cocooned in his own little world. And it's a world that is strictly forbidden ground to anyone but the closest of friends.

There has been a long-standing joke among Mauger's closest friends that they can telephone his home in the days prior to the world final and ask his wife: 'What's he like this week?' If Raye answers: 'He's

in a vile mood', then the odds are that his build-up has been precisely right!

Few people outside those within a champion's camp know the precise qualities that are needed to win a world final. Some world champions can happily project a devil-may-care attitude and will laugh and joke with the outsider. But if you spend any length of time with a champion, you quickly realise that even the most buoyant character is going through mental hell as the build-up to the world final gathers momentum. Is it any wonder? A fortune is at stake — and it can be wrenched from a rider's grasp by the failure of a mechanical part that costs a mere couple of coppers.

Mauger knows what it's like to enjoy the fruits of success. But he has also plunged to the depths of despair. He can still have nightmares about the Sunday in Poland in 1973 when the crown was in his sights — only for him to fall while trying to pass Jerzy Szczakiel in a run-off. And three years later he had a

golden opportunity to win his fifth title when, again in Poland, the carburettor bowl cracked and he stopped in his second ride. That was, incidentally, the first time in 60 world final rides that he had dropped three points because of a mechanical breakdown.

Mauger admits: 'I know why I lost the run-off against Szczakiel and I learnt something from that mistake. But there was no way I could have prevented the second mishap. Everything on my bikes is checked, checked, and checked again, but you cannot protect yourself against the one-in-a-million chance. A new chain could break the first time you use it. What you have to do at a world final is lengthen the odds in every single mechanical direction. To have your bikes right for a world final can cost a fortune, because everything needs renewing.'

Yet the real groundwork involved in a world title assault isn't always evident to either the terrace pundit or the rival. Over the years Mauger has earned himself a reputation for being the sport's ultimate professional. To many ears it is a dirty word, and there are those who would rather see a rider with a tearaway approach take all the honours. These people feel they are being cheated of a spectacle if the eventual winner is the man with the smoothest and least exciting style of all.

What is it that Mauger possesses that made him *the* rider of the late sixties and early seventies? He has a single-mindedness that can be quite alarming at times. There is only one goal — and that is to win the World Speedway Championship final. Any other awards that come along the way are only momentary watering holes on the road.

His preparation begins as soon as the speedway season opens. He will spend weeks and weeks trying out different machines and a variety of modifications to them. Often points dropped in big open meetings have proved to be the spring from which world final success has flowed.

Says Mauger: 'Normally I like to know a month or so before a world final which bikes I will be using. It's strange — all the engines and frames come from a production line and in theory there should be very little difference beween one bike and another. But it doesn't work like that. There can be quite shattering differences in the way two bikes handle, and in a world final you have to have the machine that is most suited to you. Many riders make the mistake of thinking you need the fastest bike to win a world final. But normally it isn't the fastest machine that wins the title — it's the best rider.

'Early in my career I learnt a lesson that was to help me win world championships — the most important thing is to win a race and it doesn't matter how slowly you go as long as you finish ahead of the next guy. That might sound simple, but it's amazing how many riders forget it when they get in front. All they can think about is screwing it on.

'Before I returned to ride in England I spent several seasons in Australia, and it was there that I realised it isn't necessary to keep the throttle full on from the start to the finish of a race. That was a mistake I had made in the Australian long-track championship for two years. On each occasion I was leading when I had mechanical trouble. Then in 1962 I decided I wouldn't commit the same error.

'In the final that year my main opponent was Jack Scott. I had an ESO and he was on a JAP, and when I built up the revs I pulled away and won it reasonably comfortably. I would be about 100 yards ahead of Scotty and would let him close up to 90 yards. Then I would turn on the throttle and pull out to about 110 yards and then knock it back again so that I was always 90-110 yards in front of him.

'In many championship events later on I was to use this technique, because I knew that it wasn't necessary to keep the throttle full on throughout the race. This was the period of my career which taught me to ride to win and not necessarily to ride to go fast. Since then that has always been my policy and it has brought its rewards — not in track records but in victories.'

It was that keen sense of exactly how much speed is necessary that helped Mauger to his record-equalling fifth world title in Gothenburg in 1977. 'Lucky Mauger', was the cry that echoed around the Ullevi stadium when he picked up the crown after a dramatic last race. He was trailing in third place when John Boulger and, simultaneously, Ole Olsen, slid to the ground on a vile evening of rain, slush, and wind. Mauger, needing the points to win, was far enough behind to avoid both the fallen riders, and he started in the re-run with all the psychological advantages on his side. Victory in that re-run saw him step onto the rostrum as the 1977 world champion.

Later he was to confide: 'I knew there was no way that John Boulger could get round the turn at the speed he was going. It wasn't possible in the conditions. So I deliberately dropped back, hoping to be able to take advantage of the fall that was bound to come. The plan worked.'

It's this ability to judge every inch of a race that has set Mauger apart from his rivals, and it is a facet of his make-up that only comes from experience. His preparation — both physical and mental — is all-consuming. I have seen him cut himself off from all his rivals during a world championship event and be completely unaware of what is happening around him. Often he has seemed to ignore the crowd's reaction during a pre-meeting parade, although in recent years he has developed a far freer mental attitude on a world final night. In the early days of his three successive title wins in 1968-70 he would literally not speak to a soul at a world final other than those working for him.

Perhaps the story that best illustrates Mauger's technique was the approach that his wife Raye received from a rival rider during the early seventies. An Australian with plenty of talent and a colourful reputation spent more than an hour trying to find out the real secrets of the Galloping Mauger. He probed with leading questions, but at the end of the conversation reached the conclusion that shortly before every world final the New Zealander was put under a spell by a hypnotist! Laughed Raye: 'I still think

that rider believes that Ivan gets into some sort of trance.'

Physically, Mauger always tries to reach a peak early in September to coincide with world final night. His keep-fit routine is launched early in the New Year while he is at home in New Zealand. He will spend hours every morning running across the sand dunes outside his beach house in Christchurch, and then during the British season he will take as much exercise as possible.

For long spells he trained with Manchester City soccer club and spent many hours in the gymnasium with England footballer Colin Bell when the City star was recovering from a serious knee injury that threatened his career. He will also spend hours in the local swimming baths building up the strength in his arms.

Mauger's fitness is legendary and this, more than any other factor, is the reason why he has remained a danger at the highest levels of international speedway even though he is now approaching his fortieth birthday. Early in his career he forecast: 'There is no reason why I should not become the oldest man to win a world championship.' That feat he still hopes to achieve, and today he still believes that it is possible for a rider approaching fifty years of age to become world champion.

'In the past the only thing that stopped the real riders from winning races when they were quite old was their lack of physical fitness. As long as I can keep fit I can ride a bike. You may lack something with age, but your colossal experience makes up for that.'

I can remember the startled looks on the faces of some of his pupils when Mauger held one of his early training schools. One of his regular 'tricks' was to ride every pupil's bike. But he did this without a break, jumping off one machine, quickly explaining to the rider what was wrong with it, and then roaring off on another. One day he completed — at my count — 136 laps without a break. On other occasions I have seen him ride flat out for more than a dozen laps, stopping only when the fuel ran out. Yet there are some riders in the game who complain at having to do two consecutive races in a meeting!

What are the other secrets of Mauger's phenomenal world championship record? Most of the reasons for this lie in the mind. He refuses to under-estimate any opponent, yet at the same time he will indulge in absurd 'kidology'. At Wroclaw in 1970 Mauger spent much of the practice period deliberately doing the wrong things. He knew that the East Europeans who were out to prevent him becoming the first man to win the world title for three consecutive years would be watching him intently, and he even had suspicions that a movie camera was being trained on his every move. So he started from the wrong gate positions, followed the wrong line into the turns, and generally turned in a slack-looking performance.

The psychological warfare lasted right up until the riders' parade. As the riders were hurrying about the

Left: 'Speedway is all about wheel grip.' This dramatic shot shows John Louis seeking it in vain on a slimy track surface.
Below: The nerve-racking build-up to a world final is shown by the expressions of Malcolm Simmons (far right) and Scott Autrey during the parade at Wembley in 1978.

pits putting on new tyres, Mauger sat on his toolbox and let everyone believe he was going to go out in his first race on tyres he had used during practice. It wasn't until the finalists were being introduced to the crowd that Mauger's two mechanics changed the rear wheel.

Again, that meeting highlighted the man's immense wisdom. While most riders would have been overawed at the thought of winning a third title, Mauger kept his cool and pulled off a shrewd piece of gamesmanship as he went to the line for his fourth race. Scheduled to compete in that race was Englishman Trevor Hedge, who had taken a frightful tumble earlier in the meeting. Mauger realised that if Hedge didn't take his rightful place, he would be replaced by the Polish reserve, Edmund Migos. Migos would be a danger man at any stage in a meeting, and more so when Mauger's only two remaining rivals for the title were both Poles. So Mauger persuaded Hedge to borrow his spare bike — and go to the start line. It may not have been the move that won the title for Mauger, but it certainly helped to ensure that he did not lose it.

In his autobiography, *Triple Crown Plus,* Mauger reveals that he had never been so mentally attuned to winning the world final as that night in Poland. He wrote: 'There was a longer gap than usual between the European and the world finals — nearly seven weeks — and during this time I worked myself into the mental state needed to win in Poland. Now I know that it was a particularly hard time for my wife and family, and

looking back I can see how they suffered. As the weeks went by, so my single-minded concentration intensified. I could go days and hardly speak to Raye or the children. I was building myself into such a mental attitude that one of two things would happen — I would either win the final or break completely.

'I got more and more worked up inside and undoubtedly became harder to live with. It was no easy life for Raye, but sensibly she kept a lot of her thoughts to herself and generally stood aside while I carried on in my own far-from-sweet way.'

Mechanically, Mauger has rarely indulged in the increasing practice of trying to find a 'superbike' for the final. Even in the days when riders were using nitro-methane fuel he refused to pour it into his world final tank, believing that it was such a volatile liquid that the slightest error of judgement in using it could see his hopes blown sky-high.

While he has always entrusted the preparation of his engines to former Sheffield rider Guy Allott and employed, on a full-time basis, at least one mechanic, during world final week Mauger himself spends most of his time in the workshop. At such times he is not experimenting, but checking and re-checking everything.

'There are some riders who believe the only way to win a world final is to have the fastest bike. That's a false philosophy. Speedway is all about wheel grip, and the only way to get grip is by throttle control. That's what wins world finals', Mauger will tell you.

Champion bikes

James — a big V-twin.

BSA — tested by Jack Parker.

CAN YOU imagine the start of a heat in a world final with Ole Olsen rolling up to the tapes on a Honda, Gordon Kennett lining up on a BMW, Ivan Mauger astride a Triumph and Peter Collins mounted on a Suzuki? Such was the bizarre situation in speedway's early days, when famous road bike manufacturers rushed to cater for the sensational new dirt-track market.

BSA, Norton, AJS, Velocette, James, Rudge, Douglas, Scott, Zenith, Sunbeam, Rex-Acme, Royal Enfield - these were only some of the makes on offer in the 1928-32 period.

Typical of the less successful bikes was the cumbersome V-twin James. BSA developed their speedway model from a simple single-cylinder engine, and every machine was tested on the company's own dirt track by the incomparable Jack Parker himself. Yet the roadster-based BSAs were under-powered and disappeared rapidly from the tracks, a fate that even befell the more purposeful-looking Zenith single-cylinder design.

On the other hand, some of the unconventional machines won many races. Scott's howling

Douglas — noisy and fast.

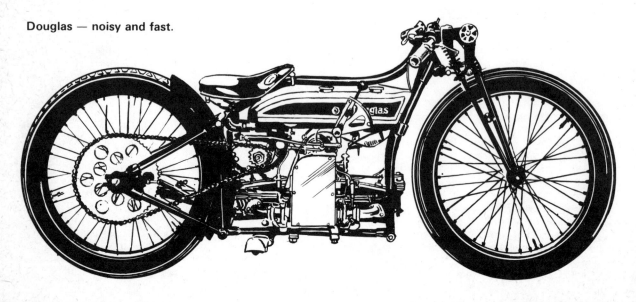

twin-cylinder bike was a water-cooled two-stroke. Frank Varey, who was later to race in two pre-war world finals, gained successes on this make in 1929. But the best-loved of the more daring designs was the Douglas flat twin. With 27 to 32 horsepower available according to the state of tune, the 'Duggie' was fast, and its fiendish din made it popular with the crowds. Riders liked it, too - 1,300 dirt-track Douglases were sold in 1929 alone.

The most futuristic of all the early speedway bikes was the Rudge, however. With its four-valve, single-cylinder engine, it pre-dated the four-valve designs of the mid-seventies by more than forty years. By 1930, the technical battle in speedway had settled down to a straight fight between the Douglas - the noisy, classic leg-trailer's machine - and the Rudge, a lighter, shorter bike that favoured less extreme riding styles. On a Rudge, Billy Lamont became the first rider to lap the Wembley oval at more than 40 mph. But within a year, both Douglas and Rudge were to be overshadowed by a new name, the JAP.

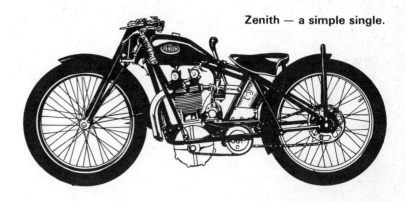

Zenith — a simple single.

Scott — two-stroke power.

Rudge — the first four-valver.

FAMOUS for their road, racing, and record-breaking engines, J A Prestwich - or JAP, as the company is always known - first produced a speedway bike in 1930. That season, Wal Phillips created a sensation by setting a new record of over 46 mph on the Stamford Bridge track, making it the fastest quarter-mile oval in Britain. A couple of months later, Phillips raised his record to 47.87 mph. JAP engineer Stanley Greening's concept of a light, low and compact single-cylinder speedway machine had paid off.

From that date JAP dominated speedway for more than three decades. Their classic 500cc engine had a long, 99mm piston stroke which gave tremendous drive on the exit from corners, and by the forties and fifties every speedway rider in the world was using JAP power.

Lionel Van Praag rode a JAP when he won the first world final in 1936. His bike gave about 38 horsepower, and JAP technology proceeded to win every world final until 1965, by which time the engine had been developed to give almost fifty horsepower.

But while JAP were celebrating, Czechoslovakia's Jawa factory launched their own speedway bike in the early sixties. A light-weight single-cylinder four-stroke, it owed much to JAP's tradition. But it had a shorter, 82mm piston stroke which allowed the engine to rev higher and thus produce more power.

Barry Briggs won the first world final for Jawa in 1966. The following year, JAP regained the championship when Ove Fundin abandoned his usual Jawa for the British machine especially for the Wembley final. But that marked the end of JAP's reign - from that time on, Jawa won every world final, and by 1968 eighty per cent of the world's speedway riders were using the Czech engine.

Then, just as Jawa had done a decade earlier, Britain's Weslake factory decided there was room for progress in speedway technology. Weslake, famous for their work with Bentley, Jaguar and their own V-12 Formula One car racing engine, were experts in packing as much fuel as possible into an engine. To achieve this in their speedway machine, they gave the engine the benefit of four valves instead of the conventional two, a move which revolutionised the sport almost overnight.

The Weslake was tested for the first time on a speedway track in 1974. The following year, it won the British League Riders championship in the hands of Peter Collins, and John Louis used one to finish third in the world final. And in 1976, Weslake ruled the world when Collins took the final in Poland.

Jawa hit back rapidly, however, and produced their own four-valver with the added sophistication of twin overhead camshafts to operate the valves. With wins in the 1977 and 1978 world finals, Jawa re-established their superiority. But the battle is now on for the eighties. JAP have produced their own twin overhead camshaft four-valve engine, and Weslake continue to improve their design. By 1978, JAP had won twenty-one world finals, Jawa eleven, and Weslake one. How will the balance of power change in the next decade?

JAP — winner of more than twenty world finals.

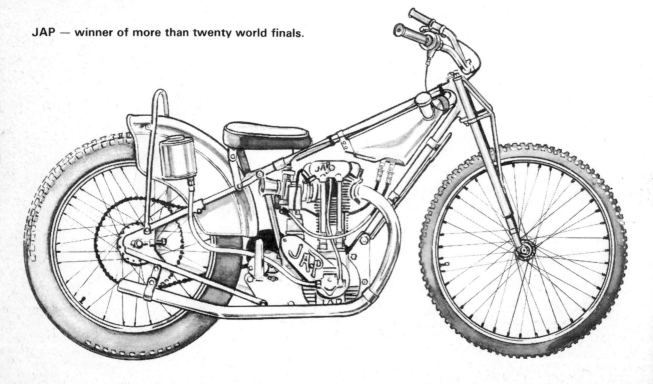

JAWA — twin overhead cam sophistication.

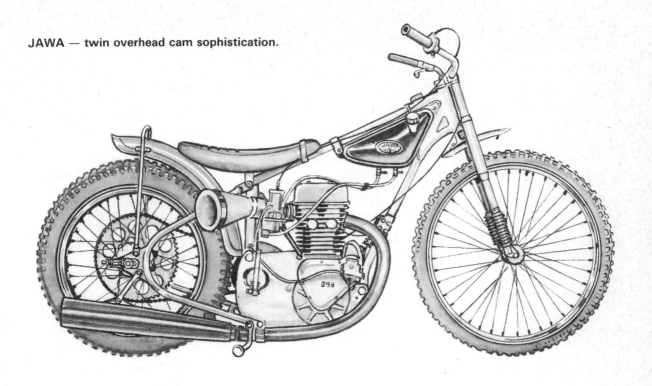

Weslake — challenger to champion in two years.

World final hall of fame

THE QUESTION has often been asked, 'Who is, or was, the greatest speedway rider of all time?' As in other sports, an answer is impossible to find. In speedway, for example, it is quite possible that the greatest ever dirt track rider was one of the early pioneers of the sport who was competing in the days before the world finals even existed. Tom Farndon was probably the most skilled rider in speedway at the time of his tragic death in 1935, a year before the inception of the world championship system. But if he had been able to compete on equal equipment with later champions such as Ove Fundin or Ivan Mauger I think he would have been capable of staying with them, and that neither of the latter would have attained the five world final victories they actually achieved. However, that opinion is pure speculation, as are the views expressed throughout this chapter, but the fact remains that it is tempting to try and evaluate the merits of the various top riders who played their parts in the history of speedway.

'Sprouts' Elder, that enigmatic American who rode during the early years of dirt track racing in Britain, used to demand from promoters the same kind of sums that today's super-stars receive, yet the changing values of money mean that Elder was in fact earning vastly more than riders of the 1970s. He is reputed to have asked for, and got, £500 to enter non-championship meetings, and I'm sure that if he had lived in a different era he would have been capable of breaking the grip that Barry Briggs, Fundin, and Mauger established on world finals.

Frank Charles was another fine rider who could well have emerged as a post-war champion, but he was killed in an air crash before war broke out. And what of the legendary Jack Parker, who still insists that he was a world champion in the early thirties when there was a proliferation of all kinds of championship meetings? Parker's talents would have been at their best during the years between 1938 and 1949, and in my mind

there is no doubt that he would have become an official world champion if the event had been staged during those years when there would have been more world class riders competing than at any other time in the history of the sport.

Among the riders who seemed to suffer from nerves on the big occasions or were dogged by injuries was Ron Johnson, the dapper little Australian who, on his day, was capable of beating the best in the world. I would love to see 'Johnno' blasting around the outside of Ivan Mauger, and I believe he could also have coped with the bustling Barry Briggs, while it would be worth travelling many miles to witness the sight of a battle between Johnson and Peter Collins.

The articulate Vic Duggan was another rider who should surely have been champion of the world, although circumstances prevented it. His undoubted ability was beyond comparison in 1947 and 1948

Jack Young at the peak of his career in 1952, holding Alan Hunt against the fence.

A line-up of great champions pictured at Wembley Bjorn Knutsson, Jack Milne, Ove Fundin and Freddie

when the world championships had been abandoned and the British Riders contest represented the ultimate speedway event. If this form could have been transferred to the Briggs, Fundin and Mauger era I'm sure that Duggan would still have won more races than he lost. Also from that period George Wilks and Alec Statham had the talent to beat the best in the world while Bill Kitchen had passed his peak by the time he qualified for the 1950 world final.

Of those who actually won finals, speedway's first world champion, Lionel Van Praag, was a hard-riding Australian who would probably have been out of his depth with the giants of the sixties and the seventies. Jack Milne was another superb rider who was robbed of his greatest moments by the Second World War, but he would have been able to hold his own with any of the all-time greats, as would his brother Cordy. Cordy was a very under-rated rider, and another whose

in 1978. From left, Tommy Price, Barry Briggs, Williams.

career would have blossomed further but for the war.

In my opinion, however, 'Bluey' Wilkinson was the greatest world champion of them all. In 10 races during the two finals he contested he dropped only one point, and bearing in mind the injuries that handicapped him during his 1938 victory, his performance was nothing short of miraculous. Although he retired from racing in 1939, I am convinced that he would have ridden in post-war speedway if he had not been killed in a road crash in 1940. If that had been possible speedway history would probably have read differently now. One statistic that underlines the ability of the red-headed Australian is that he remains the only rider to have scored a maximum in every match of a five-match test series between Australia and England. He achieved this feat during the winter of 1937-38.

Tommy Price was a toughened veteran by the time he won the world title in 1949. An accomplished rider who never knew when he was beaten, he was robbed of more major honours by the intervention of the war. The fact that during the latter part of his career he was consistently able to beat Briggs and Fundin when he was over 40 years of age is an indication of the titles he might have won but for the 11-year break in the running of world finals.

Freddie Williams is probably the most under-rated of all speedway world champions, even though he took the title twice. Criticised as having an advantage in world finals because he rode for the Wembley league side, he disproved this theory by performing well in individual events and test matches on other tracks. A fast gater and an unorthodox rider, Williams was a match for anyone on his day, and I don't think he would have been disgraced if he had been able to ride against Fundin and Mauger.

Jack Young was the greatest thing in speedway between 1950 and 1954. He was immaculate in style, virtually unbeatable on the track, and had a

The 1938 champion Bluey Wilkinson — still the greatest of them all?

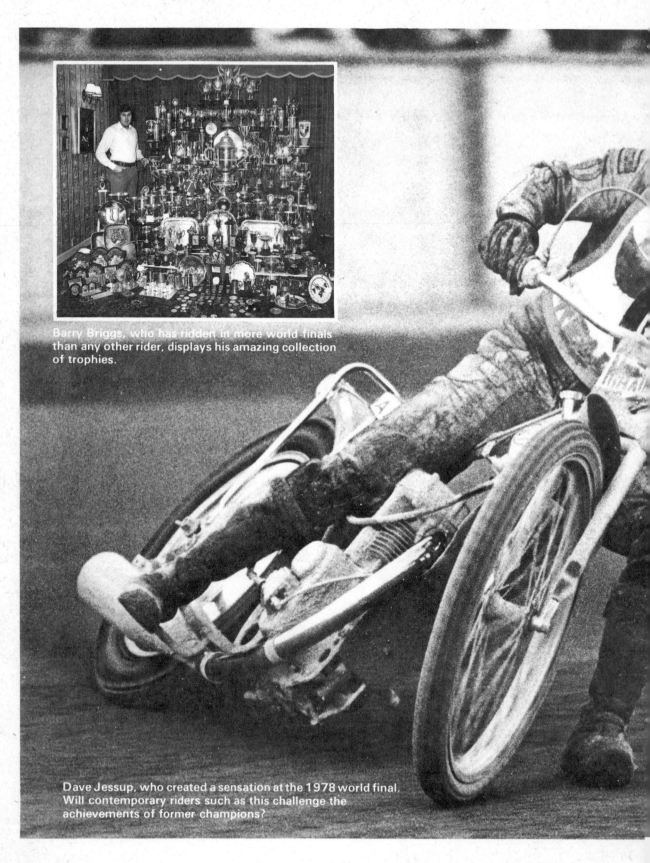

Barry Briggs, who has ridden in more world finals than any other rider, displays his amazing collection of trophies.

Dave Jessup, who created a sensation at the 1978 world final. Will contemporary riders such as this challenge the achievements of former champions?

England hero Peter Collins, one of the great riders to emerge during the 1970s.

tremendous sense of humour. Young would undoubtedly have won more than two world titles if he had been born a decade or so later and thus been able to take advantage of an era when competition was less fierce. He feared no opponent and could never be bluffed by any rider who indulged in heavy-handed tactics on the track. Young scored his world final victories at a time when he had to face opposition that was probably tougher than in any other period of speedway history.

Ronnie Moore, or 'Mirac' as he was more affectionately known, was another rider who was probably born too soon to win more than two world finals. Despite suffering many cruel injuries during his career, he was a courageous battler on the track, a worthy adversary to Fundin and Briggs, and on his best form he would have been able to challenge Ivan Mauger.

Peter Craven was the best loved champion of them all. Fans, riders, and promoters had the greatest admiration for him both as a rider and as a person, and he earned nicknames such as the 'Wizard of Balance' and the 'Mighty Atom'. I once asked Ken McKinlay, who qualified for a dozen world finals in his 27-year career, to name the opponent he had most respected during that time. Without hesitation, he replied, 'Peter Craven, because he never even thought about being unfair.' If Craven had lived into the late sixties and the early seventies there is no doubt that he would have added to his list of titles at the expense of the big three — Fundin, Briggs, and Mauger.

Fundin is said by many speedway followers to have been the greatest champion of them all, and indeed he has five world titles to back up that claim. 'Mr Perpetual Motion' was one of the nicknames he gained, but although Fundin never knew when he was beaten I think he might have had a harder time mastering Bluey Wilkinson, Tommy Price, Freddie Williams, and Jack Young when these riders were in their prime than he did in beating his contemporaries. To be fair, however, one should remember that Fundin suffered some nasty injuries at crucial times of his career, yet he stayed at the top for a period of 10 years (1956-65) during which he never finished outside the top three in world finals.

With four wins, three seconds, and three third placings, Barry Briggs has the longest running world championship record of any rider. He has scored no less than 201 points from 87 races in 18 finals, but this does not necessarily make him the greatest rider in world final history. Bluey Wilkinson and Jack Young in particular would probably have dented Briggs's reputation if they had been riding at the same time. Almost certainly, two more recent world champions, Ole Olsen and Peter Collins, would also have been able to challenge Briggs when he was at the peak of his form. I was fortunate to be able to observe Briggs at the beginning and end of his career, during which time he progressed from being a harum-scarum youth to an experienced professional. Injuries also interfered with his career, but while Briggs stands as a great

Ove Fundin stayed in the top three placings in world finals for an incredible ten years.

champion, at the time he was scoring his successes the sport was at a low ebb and competition was perhaps not as keen as it had been a decade earlier.

Bjorn Knutsson, the stylish Swede who won the 1965 world final, would almost certainly have won more titles had he not retired while at the top. In doing so, he made way for the mighty Ivan Mauger. Another five times winner of the world title, Mauger was responsible for bringing true professionalism to speedway; his dedication to winning, his immaculate equipment, and his carefully planned strategies changed the whole face of the sport he had chosen as his career. Like Fundin, Mauger managed to fill one of the first three places in world final results for almost a 10-year period (1967 to 1974), but one wonders how he would have coped with Split Waterman, Brian Crutcher, or Bluey Wilkinson. If this had happened, my guess is that Mauger would have enjoyed less success. Again, this opinion remains in the realms of conjecture, but what cannot be denied is that Wilkinson, Waterman, Craven and company were more exciting riders to watch.

So little is known about Jerzy Szczakiel, the man who in 1973 caused the biggest upset in world final history, that it would perhaps be unfair to criticise his brief career as a champion. And although Anders Michanek won the title in 1974 and was runner-up the following year, he perhaps did not need speedway enough to want to challenge for the greatest-ever tag. A rider with magnificent style, he could have emulated Fundin, but chose to do things his own way, and presumably enjoyed his speedway racing better while not possessing the dedication necessary to be ranked among the all-time greats.

Of the riders who have won world finals, that leaves us with Ole Olsen and Peter Collins, who I'm sure will win further titles in the future. In addition, the fighting style of both riders is bringing excitement back into the sport.

Could it be said from this review of great riders that Jack Parker, the man whose career began in the late twenties and ended in the fifties, is the greatest of them all? I've no doubt that the voluble Jack himself would certainly agree! But what of Max Grosskreutz, 'Tiger' Stevenson, who always seemed to be overshadowed by Bluey Wilkinson, Split Waterman, Graham Warren, Brian Crutcher, Aub Lawson, and Olle Nygren, all stalwarts of the sport and world finalists who for various reasons never quite made it to the top?

Then again, speedway followers whose memories stretch back to the sport's earliest years will no doubt regard Sprouts Elder, Vic Huxley, Jack Barnett and Wal Phillips as incomparable. There were also those riders whose careers were cut short by crashes that led either to death or serious injury. Gerald Hussey, Tom Farndon, Basse Hveem, Sverre Harrfeldt, Ernie Roccio, Valeri Klementiev, Tommy Jansson, Torbjorn Harrysson, Christer Lofqvist, George Newton, Louis Lawson, Tadeuz Teodorowicz, Brian Brett, Ken Le Breton — would they have progressed to rank among the all-time greats? The question will continue to be pondered as long as speedway is raced, but perhaps this chapter has reminded fans of contemporary stars that many of the old-time performers carry equal weight when the matter of real championship quality is considered. My personal feeling is that Bluey Wilkinson remains speedway's champion of champions when performances on world final nights are counted.

Statistical Section

The following pages form a statistical analysis of the history of the World Speedway Championship, the details being divided into three sections for ease of reference.

The opening part provides lists of the leading 40 scorers in world final history and the 40 riders who have accumulated the best averages. Riders who have appeared in only one or two world finals may tend to show up well in the table of averages, yet it would be unfair to ignore their performances. It could be said that a rider with only a couple of finals behind him had a much better chance of gaining a high average score than a contestant who had competed in several finals. However, any such complaint is offset by the accompanying list of highest scorers, which highlights the consistent performers.

The second section deals with the countries that have had representatives in world finals. Each of the 17 nations has a chart which is laid out in chronological order. In this way it is easy to note the first rider to represent a particular country, and when. It can be seen that England has the largest chart because it is the only country to have had at least one rider contesting every world final. In fact, 81 riders have appeared for England, 30 for Sweden, 24 for Australia, 24 for Poland, 14 for the USSR, seven for New Zealand, six each for the USA, Norway and Czechoslovakia, four for Wales (three of whom were the Williams brothers), three for Denmark, two each for Canada, Scotland, South Africa, West Germany and East Germany, and one for Finland. This makes a total of 216 riders who have represented the 17 countries in the 33 world finals held up to 1978.

Only 16 riders have emerged as winners from those 33 finals. Ove Fundin and Ivan Mauger have each taken the title five times, Barry Briggs has held it on four occasions, Ole Olsen is a three-times winner, Jack Young, Freddie Williams, Ronnie Moore, and the late Peter Craven have each won the title on two occasions, and the following eight riders have been successful once: Lionel Van Praag, Jack Milne, Bluey Wilkinson, Tommy Price, Bjorn Knutsson, Jerzy Szczakiel, Anders Michanek and Peter Collins.

The third statistical section comprises an analysis of the performance of every rider who has featured in world final history. If, for example, we take Joe Abbott, the man who, in alphabetical order, appears at the top of the chart, we find that he contested one final, scored six points, had no wins, scored two second places and two thirds, and was unplaced once. If he had qualified for a final as a reserve but had not been called upon to ride he would be shown to have had five 'did not rides', as is the case with Martin Ashby, a little lower down the table, who was a non-riding reserve for one of his two final appearances. The alphabetical layout of this section makes it especially easy to identify a particular favourite's efforts.

To show an example of the usefulness of this alphabetical section, it reveals that Barry Briggs rode in 87 heats in world finals, but was unplaced in only two of them, one of these being the race in which he crashed in 1972 and subsequently lost a finger. It also highlights the achievements of the also-rans: Bill Kitchen, for instance, never reached the top three in any of the four world finals that he contested, yet he was never unplaced in any of the 15 heats in which he appeared. Likewise, Ron Johnston rode in four consecutive finals without scoring major honours, yet still managed to pick up points in every one of his 20 races. The incredible Bluey Wilkinson scored nine race wins and a second place in the 10 heats that he contested in two finals, while at the other end of the scale, Ken McKinlay was reserve on three occasions in his 12 world final appearances, but was never able to make a start in any of those three years.

Many other similar facts and figures can be brought to light from a study of the entire statistical section, and hopefully will settle a host of disputed queries in speedway history. The figures may also serve as invaluable assistance on those social occasions when supporters' club organisers are staging quizzes and similar functions.

Leading Scorers 1936-78

	Points	Races	Rider	Nationality
1	201	87	Barry Briggs	New Zealand
2	173	75	Ove Fundin	Sweden
3	162	65	Ivan Mauger	New Zealand
4	143	69	Ronnie Moore	New Zealand
5	96	50	Peter Craven	England
6	95	51	Anders Michanek	Sweden
7	86	37	Ole Olsen	Denmark
8	73	44	Aub Lawson	Australia
9	70	35	Jack Young	Australia
10	66	45	Ken McKinlay	Scotland
11	64	30	Bjorn Knutsson	Sweden
12	57	30	Igor Plechanov	USSR
13	56	30	Soren Sjosten	Sweden
14	54	30	Brian Crutcher	England
	54	25	Bengt Jansson	Sweden
	54	25	Olle Nygren	Sweden
17	52	25	Peter Collins	England
18	48	25	Jack Parker	England
	48	25	Split Waterman	England
	48	20	Freddie Williams	Wales
21	47	40	Nigel Boocock	England
	47	40	Ron How	England
23	45	35	Rune Sormander	Sweden
24	42	25	Antoni Woryna	Poland
25	41	20	John Louis	England
26	40	33	Edward Jancarz	Poland
	40	20	Gote Nordin	Sweden
	40	33	Bernt Persson	Sweden
	40	25	Pawel Waloszek	Poland
30	37	25	Arthur Forrest	England
31	35	15	Wilbur Lamoreaux	USA
	35	15	Jack Milne	USA
	35	20	Zenon Plech	Poland
34	34	25	Peter Moore	Australia
35	33	20	Ron Johnston	New Zealand
	33	15	Malcolm Simmons	England
37	32	20	Tommy Price	England
38	31	15	Cordy Milne	USA
	31	14	Lionel Van Praag	Australia
40	29	10	Bluey Wilkinson	Australia

The above figures do not include the bonus points carried forward to pre-1949 world finals, or points scored in run-off heats to decide ties for the top three placings.

Leading Averages 1936-78

	Points	Rider	Nationality
1	14.50	Bluey Wilkinson	Australia
2	13.00	Wally Green	England
3	12.46	Ivan Mauger	New Zealand
4	12.00	Sverre Harrfeldt	Norway
	12.00	Gordon Kennett	England
	12.00	Bob Oakley	England
	12.00	Freddie Williams	Wales
8	11.66	Wilbur Lamoreaux	USA
	11.66	Jack Milne	USA
10	11.53	Ove Fundin	Sweden
11	11.50	Louis Lawson	England
12	11.17	Barry Briggs	New Zealand
13	11.00	Phil Crump	Australia
	11.00	Boris Samorodov	USSR
	11.00	Malcolm Simmons	England
16	10.80	Bengt Jansson	Sweden
	10.80	Olle Nygren	Sweden
18	10.75	Ole Olsen	Denmark
19	10.66	Bjorn Knutsson	Sweden
20	10.50	Michael Lee	England
21	10.40	Peter Collins	England
22	10.33	Cordy Milne	USA
	10.33	Lionel Van Praag	Australia
24	10.25	John Louis	England
25	10.21	Ronnie Moore	New Zealand
26	10.00	Gote Nordin	Sweden
	10.00	Finn Thomsen	Denmark
	10.00	Jack Young	Australia
29	9.60	Peter Craven	England
	9.60	Jack Parker	England
	9.60	Split Waterman	England
32	9.50	Hasse Holmqvist	Sweden
	9.50	Christer Lofqvist	Sweden
34	9.33	Soren Sjosten	Sweden
35	9.30	Anders Michanek	Sweden
36	9.00	Scott Autrey	USA
	9.00	Brian Brett	England
	9.00	Brian Crutcher	England
	9.00	Bill Kitchen	England
40	8.75	Zenon Plech	Poland

The above figures do not include the bonus points carried forward to pre-1949 world finals, or points scored in run-off heats to decide ties for the top three placings. A final for which a rider qualified as a reserve has also not been counted, whether or not he was able to complete some rides in the meeting.

Country-by-country

The figures below do not include the bonus points carried forward to pre-1949 world finals, or points scored in run-off heats to decide ties for the top three placings. * indicates a rider who qualified for the 1939 final, which was not run. + indicates a rider who qualified for a final as a reserve, but was not called upon to ride. +3 indicates a reserve who was called upon to ride: figure beside plus sign indicates his score.

Points	Finals	Rider	1936	37	38	39	49	50	51	52	53	54	55	56	57	58	59	60	61	62	63	64	65	66	67	68	69	70	71	72	73	74	75	76	77	78
Australia																																			
31	4	Lionel Van Praag	14	6	11	*																														
29	2	Bluey Wilkinson	15	14																																
8	1	Dicky Case	8																																	
7	1	Vic Huxley	7																																	
4	2	Vic Duggan			*	4																														
—	2	Ron Johnson		+	*																															
73	10	Aub Lawson				*	8	10	7	7	4			11	11	11	4																			
8	1	Bill Longley				8																														
27	4	Graham Warren				5	12			5	5																									
4	1	Ken Le Breton				4																														
1	1	Cliff Watson				1																														
70	8	Jack Young					7	12	14	10	11	10						6																		
24	6	Jack Biggs					3	12		2	7			+	+																					
9	3	Arthur Payne					0	7		9	+																									
7	1	Bob Leverenz						7																												
34	5	Peter Moore												8		5	3	12		6																
10	2	Jack Geran													7	3																				
5	1	Chum Taylor															5																			
3	1	Ray Cresp																	3																	
8	1	Jim Airey																										8								
11	2	John Boulger																												6				5		
22	2	Phil Crump																														10	12			
6	1	Billy Sanders																																6		
7	1	John Titman																																		7
Canada																																			
4	2	Eric Chitty	4		*																															
—	1	Jimmy Gibb		+																																

Points	Finals	Rider	1936	37	38	39	49	50	51	52	53	54	55	56	57	58	59	60	61	62	63	64	65	66	67	68	69	70	71	72	73	74	75	76	77	78
Czechoslovakia																																				
—	**	Antonin Kasper																			**															
3	1	Jaroslav Wolf																				3														
2	1	Lubos Tomicek																				2														
14	4	Jiri Stancl																										3					6	3		2
6	2	Jan Verner																																1	5	
0	1	Petra Ondrasik																																	0	
—	1	Zdenek Kudrna																																	+	
Denmark																																				
13	2	Morian Hansen		5	8																																
86	6	Ole Olsen																									6	15	12	11	2	15	12	13		
10	1	Finn Thomsen																																10		
East Germany																																				
0	1	Jochen Dinse																								0										
5	1	Hans Jurgen Fritz																										5								
England																																				
25	4	Eric Langton	13	4	8	*																															
15	2	Frank Charles	8	7																																	
13	2	Jack Ormston	8		+5																																
11	3	George Newton	4	5	2																																
5	1	Bob Harrison	5																																		
5	1	Wal Phillips	5																																		
13	2	Ginger Lees	4	9																																	
14	4	Arthur Atkinson	3	6	5	*																															
2	1	Bill Pitcher	2																																		
48	7	Jack Parker	#	10	6	*	*	14	8	10																										
6	1	Joe Abbott		6																																	
3	3	Frank Varey		3	0	*																															
6	2	Tommy Croombs		2	4																																
8	4	Alec Statham		+0	8	+																															
32	4	Tommy Price			4			15	8			5																									
2	1	Geoff Pymar			2																																
—	1	Eric Collins				*																															

**Antonin Kasper qualified as reserve for Czechoslovakia in 1963 but did not appear.   # Jack Parker qualified in 1936 but was injured and unfit to compete.

Country-by-country

The figures below do not include the bonus points carried forward to pre-1949 world finals, or points scored in run-off heats to decide ties for the top three placings. *indicates a rider who qualified for the 1939 final, which was not run. † indicates a rider who qualified for a final as a reserve, but was not called upon to ride. +3 indicates a reserve who was called upon to ride. figure beside plus sign indicates his score.

England continued

Points	Finals	Rider	1936	37	38	39	49	50	51	52	53	54	55	56	57	58	59	60	61	62	63	64	65	66	67	68	69	70	71	72	73	74	75	76	77	78
23	3	Louis Lawson					13	10		+																										
27	4	Bill Kitchen		9	9	*	9																													
1	1	Oliver Hart				+1																														
14	3	Norman Parker			+1		10	3																												
11	2	Ron Clarke					8	3																												
14	5	Cyril Roger					7	+5	2				0				0																			
6	1	Bill Gilbert					6																													
2	1	Lloyd Goffe					2																													
7	3	Dent Oliver					0	6			+1																									
13	1	Wally Green					13																													
48	5	Split Waterman					8	12	6	13	9																									
10	2	Cyril Brine					7	3																												
5	1	Danny Dunton					5																													
0	1	Mike Erskine					+0																													
15	2	Eddie Rigg						8			7																									
21	3	Jeff Lloyd						6	7	8																										
11	4	Alan Hunt						2		3	+			6																						
13	3	Dick Bradley						+2	9	2																										
12	1	Bob Oakley							12																											
37	5	Arthur Forrest						7		7	5	7	11																							
54	8	Brian Crutcher						6	6	13	10	9			+	+	10																			
4	1	Derek Close								4																										
47	9	Ron How							0				7	7	7	3	‡	7	6	7	10															
7	1	Fred Brand									7																									
96	10	Peter Craven										3	13	11	11	7	11	14	6	14	6															
6	1	Billy Bales											6																							
6	1	Arthur Wright											6																							
2	1	Phil Clarke											2																							
7	3	Gerald Hussey										+	0			7																				
7	1	Eric Boothroyd											7																							

‡ Ron How qualified in 1960 but was injured and unfit to compete.

138

Points	Finals	Rider	1936	37	38	39	49	50	51	52	53	54	55	56	57	58	59	60	61	62	63	64	65	66	67	68	69	70	71	72	73	74	75	76	77	78
11	3	Dick Fisher											5																							
47	10	Nigel Boocock												+						5	1	8	6	8	2	1	10		6							
8	1	Bob Roger													8																					
11	2	George White													4		7																			
19	7	Mike Broadbanks														5			2	2		6	+	4	+											
0	1	Bryan Elliott																0																		
25	4	Bob Andrews																+	2	10	9	4														
12	2	Cyril Maidment																			8	4														
2	2	Ron Mountford																		2	+															
4	2	Jim Lightfoot																			4	+														
—	1	Tadeusz Teodorowicz																																		
9	1	Brian Brett																					9													
5	1	Reg Luckhurst																					5													
3	1	Jimmy Gooch																					3													
15	3	Eric Boocock																						9	4				2							
28	4	Ray Wilson																						7	11					5		5				
5	1	Rick France																							5											
4	1	Colin Pratt																							4											
5	2	Martin Ashby																								5					+					
1	1	Howard Cole																									1									
—	1	Arnold Haley																									+									
0	1	Trevor Hedge																										0								
—	1	Tony Lomas																											+							
41	4	John Louis																												11	9	9	12			
52	5	Peter Collins																													6	9	10	14	13	
6	1	Terry Betts																														6				
16	2	Dave Jessup																														5				11
33	3	Malcolm Simmons																															10	13	10	
8	1	Doug Wyer																																8		
6	1	Chris Morton																																6		
21	2	Michael Lee																																	12	9
—	1	John Davis																																	+	
12	1	Gordon Kennett																																		12
—	1	Steve Bastable																																		+

Country-by-country

The figures below do not include the bonus points carried forward to pre-1949 world finals, or points scored in run-off heats to decide ties for the top three placings. * indicates a rider who qualified for the 1939 final, which was not run. + indicates a rider who qualified for a final as a reserve, but was not called upon to ride. +3 indicates a reserve who was called upon to ride; figure beside plus sign indicates his score.

Points	Finals	Rider	1936	37	38	39	49	50	51	52	53	54	55	56	57	58	59	60	61	62	63	64	65	66	67	68	69	70	71	72	73	74	75	76	77	78
Finland																																			
6	1	Ila Teromaa																																	6	
New Zealand																																			
143	14	Ronnie Moore						7	11	10	9	15	12	12		9	15	14	10	9						6			4							
23	4	Geoff Mardon						+		12	5						6																			
5	2	Trevor Redmond							+		5	5																								
—	1	Maury Dunn								+																										
201	18	Barry Briggs									9	12	10	14	15	11	9	12	13	12	15	10	15	11	12	11	7		3							
33	4	Ron Johnston											6			9	8	10																		
162	13	Ivan Mauger																				11	13	15	14	15	12		13	13	11	12	11	14		8
Norway																																			
2	1	Henry Andersen											2																							
—	1	Basse Hveem								+																										
4	1	Aage Hansen													4																					
24	2	Sverre Harrfeldt																			10			14												
3	1	Reidar Eide																								3										
6	1	Dag Lovaas																														6				
Poland																																			
5	2	Mieczyslaw Polukard															5	+																		
8	2	Florian Kapala															+	8																		
6	2	Marian Kaiser																1						5												
4	3	Henryk Zyto																4		+										+						
8	1	Stefan Kwoczala																8																		
10	2	Stanislaw Tkocz																3							7											
40	5	Pawel Waloszek																		2						10		14	6	8						
6	2	Zbigniew Podlecki																				3					+3									
17	6	Andrzej Wyglenda																				4	2		2		2	7		+0						
25	4	Andrzej Pogorzelski																				7	5	6			7									

140

Points	Finals	Rider	1936	37	38	39	49	50	51	52	53	54	55	56	57	58	59	60	61	62	63	64	65	66	67	68	69	70	71	72	73	74	75	76	77	78
42	5	Antoni Woryna																					6	13	5	5	13									
—	1	Marian Rose																						+												
6	2	Jerzy Trzeskowski																							3	3										
40	7	Edward Jancarz																								11	9				6	+1	4	5	4	
—	1	Jerzy Padewski																								+										
21	4	Jan Mucha																									7				7				1	
14	3	Henryk Glucklich																									5	9				0				
2	1	Zygfryd Friedek																										2								
4	1	Edmund Migos																										+4								
13	3	Jerzy Szczakiel																											+	0	13					
35	4	Zenon Plech																													12	8	4	11		
10	3	Marek Cieslak																															1	4		5
14	2	Jerzy Rembas																															3	3		11
—	1	Boguslaw Nowak																																+		
Scotland																																			
66	12	Ken McKinlay											+	10	8	11	+	6	5	9	6	4	+			7										
2	1	Jim McMillan																												+2						
South Africa																																			
7	1	Henry Long								7																										
4	2	Doug Davies											**	4																						
Sweden																																			
11	2	Dan Forsberg								9					2																					
45	7	Rune Sormander										5			11	4	6	5	7	7																
54	5	Olle Nygren									12	13	9			9	11																			
173	15	Ove Fundin										2	10	13	14	13	13	14	10	14	13	13	13		14	7	9									
3	1	Kjell Carlsson											3																							
23	5	Peo Soderman												10	7	+					5			1												
2	1	Ulf Ericsson												2																						
2	1	Olle Andersson II												2																						
0	1	Joel Jansson														0																				
12	3	Arne Carlsson															8			3		1														
40	6	Gote Nordin																	12	9	10	+		9					+							
56	6	Soren Sjosten																	8			9					11	9	8							

**Doug Davies qualified for the 1955 world final but had to withdraw because of illness.

Country-by-country

The figures below do not include the bonus points carried forward to pre-1949 world finals, or points scored in run-off heats to decide ties for the top three placings. *indicates a rider who qualified for the 1939 final, which was not run. + indicates a rider who qualified for a final as a reserve, but was not called upon to ride. +3 indicates a reserve who was called upon to ride. figure beside plus sign indicates his score.

Points	Finals	Rider	1936	37	38	39	49	50	51	52	53	54	55	56	57	58	59	60	61	62	63	64	65	66	67	68	69	70	71	72	73	74	75	76	77	78
		Sweden continued																																		
64	6	Bjorn Knutsson																12	10	13	10	14	5													
1	1	Per Tage Svensson																			1															
8	2	Leif Larsson																					5	3												
54	5	Bengt Jansson																				10	14					12			9			9		
24	3	Torbjorn Harrysson																						10	10	4										
12	3	Leif Enecrona																						8	+			4								
—	1	Bengt Brannefors																						+												
40	8	Bernt Persson																						6	1			9	13	0		5		6		
95	11	Anders Michanek																						9	9			7	11	8	6	15	13+2		8	7
7	1	Gunnar Malmqvist																							7											
19	2	Hasse Holmqvist																								9	10									
11	4	Tommy Jansson																										1			+	+3	7			
19	2	Christer Lofqvist																											11		8					
2	1	Jan Simensen																												+2						
8	1	Tommy Johansson																													8					
6	1	Tommy Nilsson																																6		
—	1	Soren Karlsson																																	+	
3	1	Jan Andersson																																		3
		USA																																		
31	4	Cordy Milne	11	12	8	*																														
35	4	Jack Milne	6	15	14	*																														
35	4	Wilbur Lamoreaux	13	13	*	9																														
7	2	Benny Kaufman			7	*																														
2	1	Ernie Roccio						2																												
18	2	Scott Autrey																														7				11

142

Points	Finals	Rider	1936	37	38	39	49	50	51	52	53	54	55	56	57	58	59	60	61	62	63	64	65	66	67	68	69	70	71	72	73	74	75	76	77	78
		USSR																																		
57	7	Igor Plechanov																	4	7		13	13	8	12	+										
20	3	Gennady Kurilenko																							11			2								
22	2	Boris Samorodov																			11	11						4	8								
12	2	Valeri Klementiev																										5		2	7		4	1		
19	5	Valeri Gordeev																											11			0	0	0		
11	4	Vladimir Gordeev																												4	10	6		+		
20	4	Grigori Chlynovski																												8			8			
8	1	Alexander Pavlov																												6						
14	2	Viktor Trofimov																												6						
6	1	Viktor Kalmykov																												4						
4	1	Anatoli Kuzmin																													8					
8	1	Vladimir Paznikov																													2					
2	1	Vladimir Zapleczny																														3				
3	1	Mikhail Kraznov																																		
		Wales																																		
48	5	Freddie Williams					14	7	13	14	+																									
22	4	Eric Williams							6	4			12					**																		
3	1	Ian Williams													3																					
7	1	Leo McAuliffe																		7																
		West Germany																																		
12	4	Josef Hofmeister														0	2	4	6																	
16	2	Egon Muller																																8	8	

** Eric Williams qualified for the 1960 world final but had to withdraw for domestic reasons.

A complete alphabetical listing of riders who have qualified for world finals from 1936 to 1978, with

Rider	Finals	Points	1st	2nd	3rd	Unplaced	Did not ride
Joe Abbott	1	6	0	2	2	1	—
Jim Airey	1	8	1	2	1	1	—
Henry Andersen	1	2	0	0	2	3	—
Jan Andersson	1	3	0	0	3	2	—
Olle Andersson	1	2	0	0	2	3	—
Bob Andrews	4	25	2	8	3	3	4
Martin Ashby	2	5	0	2	1	2	5
Arthur Atkinson	4	14	0	4	6	5	5*
Scott Autrey	2	18	2	5	2	1	—
Billy Bales	1	6	0	2	2	1	—
Steve Bastable	1	—	—	—	—	—	5
Terry Betts	1	6	1	0	3	1	—
Jack Biggs	6	24	5	1	7	6	11
Eric Boocock	3	15	2	3	3	7	—
Nigel Boocock	10	47	6	8	13	13	10
Eric Boothroyd	1	7	1	1	2	1	—
John Boulger	2	11	0	4	3	3	—
Dick Bradley	3	13	2	3	1	5	4
Fred Brand	1	7	1	1	2	1	—
Bengt Brannefors	1	—	—	—	—	—	5
Brian Brett	1	9	2	1	1	1	—
Barry Briggs	18	201	47	22	16	2	3
Cyril Brine	2	10	0	4	2	4	—
Mike Broadbanks	7	19	1	4	8	12	10
Arne Carlsson	3	12	1	1	7	6	—
Kjell Carlsson	1	3	0	1	1	3	—
Dicky Case	1	8	1	2	1	1	—
Frank Charles	2	15	4	1	1	4	—
Eric Chitty	2	4	0	1	2	2	5*
Grigori Chlynovski	4	20	3	4	3	5	5
Marek Cieslak	3	10	1	1	5	8	—
Phil Clarke	1	2	0	1	0	4	—
Ron Clarke	2	11	1	3	2	4	—
Derek Close	1	4	0	1	2	2	—
Howard Cole	1	1	0	0	1	4	—
Eric Collins	1	—	—	—	—	—	5*
Peter Collins	5	52	11	8	3	3	—
Peter Craven	10	96	21	14	5	10	—
Ray Cresp	1	3	0	1	1	3	—
Tommy Croombs	2	6	0	1	4	5	—
Phil Crump	2	22	5	2	3	0	—
Brian Crutcher	8	54	9	9	9	3	10
Doug Davies	2	4	0	1	2	2	5
John Davis	1	—	—	—	—	—	5
Jochen Dinse	1	0	0	0	0	5	—
Vic Duggan	2	4	0	0	4	1	5*
Maury Dunn	1	—	—	—	—	—	5
Danny Dunton	1	5	0	1	3	1	—
Reidar Eide	1	3	0	1	1	3	—
Bryan Elliott	1	0	0	0	0	4	1
Leif Enecrona	3	12	0	5	2	3	5
Ulf Ericsson	1	2	0	0	2	3	—
Mike Erskine	1	0	—	—	—	1	4
Dick Fisher	3	11	0	3	5	7	—
Arthur Forrest	5	37	6	6	7	6	—
Dan Forsberg	2	11	2	1	3	4	—
Rick France	1	5	0	1	3	1	—
Zygfryd Friedek	1	2	0	1	0	3	1
Hans Jurgen Fritz	1	5	0	1	3	1	—
Ove Fundin	15	173	44	17	7	7	—
Jack Geran	2	10	1	0	7	2	—
Jimmy Gibb	1	—	—	—	—	—	5
Bill Gilbert	1	6	1	1	1	2	—
Henryk Glucklich	3	14	2	4	0	9	—
Lloyd Goffe	1	2	0	0	2	3	—
Jimmy Gooch	1	3	0	0	3	2	—
Valeri Gordeev	5	19	1	3	10	11	—
Vladimir Gordeev	4	11	2	2	1	8	7
Wally Green	1	13	3	2	0	0	—
Arnold Haley	1	—	—	—	—	—	5
Aage Hansen	1	4	0	2	0	3	—
Morian Hansen	2	13	1	3	4	2	—
Sverre Harrfeldt	2	24	5	4	1	0	—
Bob Harrison	2	5	1	1	0	3	5
Torbjorn Harrysson	3	24	2	8	2	1	2
Oliver Hart	1	1	0	0	1	2	2

The above figures do not include the bonus points carried forward to pre-1949 world finals, or points scored in run-off heats to decide ties for the top three placings.
*indicates a rider who qualified for the 1939 final, which was not run.

World Final A-Z

the number of finals contested, points scored and heat placings shown in detail.

Rider	Finals	Points	1st	2nd	3rd	Unplaced	Did not ride
Trevor Hedge	1	0	0	0	0	4	1
Josef Hofmeister	4	12	2	1	4	13	—
Hasse Holmqvist	2	19	1	7	2	0	—
Ron How	8	47	3	14	10	13	—
Alan Hunt	4	11	1	1	6	7	5
Gerald Hussey	3	7	0	3	1	6	5
Vic Huxley	1	7	0	3	1	1	—
Basse Hveem	1	—	—	—	—	—	5
Edward Jancarz	7	40	6	3	16	8	2
Bengt Jansson	5	54	11	8	5	1	—
Joel Jansson	1	0	0	0	0	0	5
Tommy Jansson	4	11	0	4	3	7	6
Dave Jessup	2	16	3	3	1	3	—
Tommy Johansson	1	8	2	1	0	2	—
Ron Johnson	2	—	—	—	—	—	10*
Ron Johnston	4	33	3	7	10	0	—
Marian Kaiser	2	6	1	0	3	6	—
Viktor Kalmykov	1	6	0	1	4	0	—
Florian Kapala	2	8	1	2	1	1	5
Soren Karlsson	1	—	—	—	—	—	5
Benny Kaufman	2	7	0	3	1	1	5*
Gordon Kennett	1	12	2	3	0	0	—
Bill Kitchen	4	27	1	10	4	0	5*
Valeri Klementiev	2	12	3	0	3	4	—
Bjorn Knutsson	6	64	17	4	5	4	—
Stefan Kwoczala	1	8	1	1	3	0	—
Mikhail Kraznov	1	3	0	0	3	2	—
Zdenek Kudrna	1	—	—	—	—	—	5
Gennady Kurilenko	3	20	3	4	3	3	2
Anatoli Kuzmin	1	4	1	0	1	3	—
Wilbur Lamoreaux	4	35	9	3	2	1	5*
Eric Langton	4	25	5	4	2	4	5*
Leif Larsson	3	8	0	3	2	5	5
Aub Lawson	10	73	10	14	15	6	5*
Louis Lawson	3	23	5	4	0	1	5
Ken Le Breton	1	4	0	0	4	1	—
Michael Lee	2	21	4	4	1	1	—
Ginger Lees	2	13	1	3	4	2	—
Bob Leverenz	1	7	1	1	2	1	—
Jim Lightfoot	2	4	0	1	2	2	5
Jeff Lloyd	3	21	2	5	5	3	—
Christer Lofqvist	2	19	4	3	1	2	—
Tony Lomas	1	—	—	—	—	—	5
Henry Long	1	7	0	3	1	1	—
Bill Longley	1	8	0	3	2	0	—
John Louis	4	41	7	8	4	1	—
Dag Lovaas	1	6	1	0	3	1	—
Reg Luckhurst	1	5	0	1	3	1	—
Leo McAuliffe	1	7	1	2	0	2	—
Ken McKinlay	12	66	10	14	8	13	15
Jim McMillan	1	2	0	—	2	—	3
Cyril Maidment	2	12	1	2	5	2	—
Gunnar Malmqvist	1	7	1	1	2	1	—
Geoff Mardon	4	23	4	4	3	4	5
Ivan Mauger	13	162	42	16	4	3	—
Anders Michanek	11	95	16	20	7	8	4
Edmund Migos	1	4	0	1	2	2	—
Cordy Milne	4	31	6	5	3	1	5*
Jack Milne	4	35	9	3	2	1	5*
Peter Moore	5	34	3	8	9	5	—
Ronnie Moore	14	143	30	21	11	8	—
Chris Morton	1	6	0	1	4	0	—
Ron Mountford	2	2	0	0	2	3	5
Jan Mucha	4	21	0	7	7	6	—
Egon Muller	2	16	3	3	1	0	—
George Newton	3	11	2	1	3	9	—
Tommy Nilsson	1	6	0	3	0	2	—
Gote Nordin	6	40	6	9	4	1	10
Boguslaw Nowak	1	—	—	—	—	—	5
Olle Nygren	5	54	9	13	1	2	—
Bob Oakley	1	12	3	1	1	0	—
Dent Oliver	3	7	1	1	2	4	7
Ole Olsen	8	86	23	7	3	4	3
Petra Ondrasik	1	0	0	0	0	5	—
Jack Ormston	2	13	2	2	3	0	3
Jerzy Padewski	1	—	—	—	—	—	5

The above figures do not include the bonus points carried forward to pre-1949 world finals, or points scored in run-off heats to decide ties for the top three placings.
*indicates a rider who qualified for the 1939 final, which was not run.

World Final A-Z

Rider	Finals	Points	1st	2nd	3rd	Unplaced	Did not ride
Jack Parker	7	48	9	9	3	4	10*
Norman Parker	3	14	2	2	4	3	4
Alexander Pavlov	1	8	2	0	2	1	—
Arthur Payne	3	9	2	1	1	6	5
Vladimir Paznikov	1	8	1	1	3	0	—
Bernt Persson	8	40	4	9	10	10	7
Wal Phillips	1	5	0	1	3	1	—
Bill Pitcher	1	2	0	0	2	3	—
Igor Plechanov	7	57	10	9	9	2	5
Zenon Plech	4	35	5	7	6	2	—
Zbigniew Podlecki	2	6	0	2	2	3	3
Andrzej Pogorzelski	4	25	2	7	5	6	—
Mieczyslaw Polukard	2	5	0	2	1	2	5
Colin Pratt	1	4	1	0	1	3	—
Tommy Price	4	32	7	3	5	5	—
Geoff Pymar	1	2	0	0	2	3	—
Trevor Redmond	2	5	0	1	3	1	5
Jerzy Rembas	2	14	3	1	3	3	—
Eddie Rigg	2	15	3	2	2	3	—
Ernie Roccio	1	2	0	1	0	3	1
Bob Roger	1	8	0	3	2	0	—
Cyril Roger	5	14	2	2	4	14	3
Marian Rose	1	—	—	—	—	—	5
Boris Samorodov	2	22	5	3	1	1	—
Billy Sanders	1	6	1	1	1	2	—
Jan Simensen	1	2	—	1	—	1	3
Malcolm Simmons	3	33	4	10	1	0	—
Soren Sjosten	6	56	11	8	7	4	—
Peo Soderman	5	23	3	5	4	8	5
Rune Sormander	7	45	4	10	13	8	—
Jiri Stancl	4	14	0	3	8	9	—
Alec Statham	4	8	2	1	0	3	14*
Per Tage Svensson	1	1	0	0	1	4	—
Jerzy Szczakiel	3	13	3	2	0	5	5
Chum Taylor	1	5	1	1	0	3	—
Tadeusz Teodorowicz	1	—	—	—	—	—	5
Ila Teromaa	1	6	1	1	1	2	—
Finn Thomsen	1	10	2	1	2	0	—
John Titman	1	7	1	1	2	1	—
Stanislaw Tkocz	2	10	1	2	3	4	—
Lubos Tomicek	1	2	0	0	2	3	—
Viktor Trofimov	2	14	0	6	2	2	—
Jerzy Trzeskowski	2	6	0	2	2	6	—
Lionel Van Praag	4	31	8	3	1	2	6*
Frank Varey	3	3	0	0	3	5	7*
Jan Verner	2	6	0	1	4	5	—
Pawel Waloszek	5	40	8	4	8	5	—
Graham Warren	4	27	4	5	5	6	—
Split Waterman	5	48	9	6	9	1	—
Cliff Watson	1	1	0	0	1	4	—
George White	2	11	1	2	4	3	—
Eric Williams	3	22	3	3	7	2	—
Freddie Williams	5	48	12	5	2	1	5
Ian Williams	1	3	0	1	1	3	—
Bluey Wilkinson	2	29	9	1	0	0	—
Ray Wilson	4	28	5	4	5	6	—
Jaroslav Wolf	1	3	0	0	3	2	—
Antoni Woryna	5	42	7	6	9	3	—
Arthur Wright	1	6	1	0	3	1	—
Doug Wyer	1	8	2	0	2	1	—
Andrzej Wyglenda	6	17	1	3	8	14	4
Jack Young	8	70	14	10	8	3	5
Vladimir Zapleczny	1	2	0	0	2	3	—
Henryk Zyto	3	4	0	1	2	2	10

The above figures do not include the bonus points carried forward to pre-1949 world finals, or points scored in run-off heats to decide ties for the top three placings.
*indicates a rider who qualified for the 1939 final, which was not run.

Did you know ?

In the 33 world finals raced between 1936 and 1978, only 13 maximums have been scored, one of which did not win the title. This was of course the famous Bluey Wilkinson 15-pointer in 1936, when he was robbed of the championship by the bonus points system then in use.

The riders who gained maximum scores in world finals are listed below, and the chart underlines the remarkable fact that Ove Fundin won the title five times without ever managing to achieve an unbeaten score:

1936	Bluey Wilkinson
1937	Jack Milne
1949	Tommy Price
1954	Ronnie Moore
1958	Barry Briggs
1959	Ronnie Moore
1964	Barry Briggs
1966	Barry Briggs
1968	Ivan Mauger
1970	Ivan Mauger
1971	Ole Olsen
1974	Anders Michanek
1975	Ole Olsen

Ronnie Moore achieved the notable feat of recording maximums on the two occasions that he won the title, while Barry Briggs put together three maximums in winning his four titles. The only rider ever to have taken a point from Briggs in his four winning years was Australian Jack Geran, who beat the multiple champion in one heat in 1957.

☐ The number 13 is popularly supposed to be unlucky, yet three riders won the world championship when carrying this number. They were Bluey Wilkinson (1938), Tommy Price (1949) and Ronnie Moore (1959). However, Jack Biggs was wearing No 13 when he should have taken the title in 1951, so maybe there is some ground for superstition after all.

☐ The luckiest numbers in world championship history are 2, 6, 10 and 14, each having carried riders to victory on four occasions. Numbers 11 and 13 have each accompanied the winners on three occasions, numbers 4, 7 and 16 have been victorious twice, and numbers 1, 8, 9, 12 and 15 have been worn by champions only once. Thus the 'unlucky' numbers are 3 and 5 — no rider carrying either of these on his back has won the title.

☐ Ole Olsen's third place in 1977 gave Coventry a representative in the top three for the first time in the history of world finals.

☐ Of the 17 nations that have contested world finals since 1936, England is the only country to have had a rider in every event.

☐ Poland have been represented in world finals every year since 1959, with the exception of 1963. In that season Polish-born Tadeuz Teodorowicz was the English reserve — he had become a naturalised Briton after choosing to stay in this country when he was a member of a Polish touring side in an earlier season.

☐ Jack Young's 12 points in 1951 stands as the lowest score to have won a world final. He followed this, however, with 14 points in 1952, to become the first rider to win in consecutive seasons.

☐ Bluey Wilkinson retired after winning the world championsip in 1938 to become a promoter at Sheffield. He had considered promoting at Ipswich, as his great friend Max Grosskreutz was riding at nearby Norwich at the time.

☐ Although there were five Australians in the 1949 final, Aub Lawson was the only one of them to win a race.

☐ Jim Boyd won the Walthamstow qualifying round for three years in 1949, '50, and '51, but never progressed beyond the next round.

☐ On the day of the 1936 world final at Wembley, BBC radio erroneously broadcast that the meeting had been cancelled. The mistake had to be put right with announcements at 15-minute intervals throughout the day.

☐ Tommy Price, the Wembley heat leader, was not seeded direct into the championship qualifying rounds in 1949. He first had to race in the eliminators on Second Division tracks, and thus had to contest five meetings before he could take the world title.

☐ The first Continental rider to gain a place in a world final was the Dane Morian Hansen, who appeared at Wembley in 1936 and '37. The next Continental to reach a final was Sweden's Dan Forsberg in 1952. He was competing in British League racing for Birmingham at the time.

☐ Sverre Harrfeldt is the only Norwegian to have finished in the first three in a world final, when he was second in 1966. He may well have gone on to equal or improve on that performance, but a serious injury in a later European final marred his career.

☐ Cyril Maidment rode at Wembley on a world final night and yet never contested a Wembley world final. This riddle is explained by the fact that he was a member of the Royal Signals display team that provided additional entertainment for the fans in 1950. Maidment did actually race in two finals, however, both times when the event was held in Sweden.

☐ Freddie Williams was still using a provisional licence on the road when he won the world championship in 1950. He later passed his motorcycle test.

☐ Jimmy Gooch, a member of the famous Wembley Lions league team in the fifties, had to wait until 1965 before he could ride in a final on his 'home' track. But by that time Wembley had long since closed as a league venue, and Gooch had ridden for a few other tracks in the intervening years.

☐ Two Irish riders who rode for First Division teams but never made a world final were Eric French and Dom Perry. They were heat leaders for New Cross and Wimbledon respectively, and French moved on to the Wembley league side when New Cross closed in the fifties.

They nearly made it

SO OFTEN it is taken for granted that the big names in speedway have ridden in the World Championship. But that assumption is only partly correct, for while the preliminary qualifying rounds are open to quite mediocre riders, some of the sport's better known personalities have not managed to fight through to an actual world final.

Many of the queries asked of me while I was compiling this book concerned the supposed world final performances of these popular men who, as it turned out when the records were consulted, had never qualified for the event. So I decided to make the following list of these great riders of the past three or four decades who missed out on speedway's greatest occasion.

Many of the finest performers in the late twenties and early thirties had, of course, retired by the time the world finals were instituted, and therefore I have omitted names such as Jack Barnett and Syd Edmonds. I have also restricted the list to riders who performed regularly on British or Australasian tracks, as almost every serious would-be world finalist has had to gain experience on these ovals. I'm sure the list will surprise many speedway followers when they consider that none of these riders has ever qualified for a world final:

Norman Hunter

Neil Street

Bob Kilby

Ivor Brown

Bruce Abernethy (New Zealand)
Oyvind Berg (Norway)
Ivor Brown (England)
Squibb Burton (England)
Johnny Chamberlain
(Australia)
Pat Clarke (England)
Norman Clay (Australia) †
Malcolm Craven (England) *
Frank Dolan (Australia)
Bob Duckworth (New Zealand)
Ray Duggan (Australia)
Sprouts Elder (USA)
Eric French (Ireland)
Ronnie Genz (England)
Colin Gooddy (England)
George Greenwood (England)
Max Grosskreutz (Australia)
Keith Gurtner (Australia)
Merv Harding (Australia)
Billy Hole (England)
Norman Hunter (England)
George Hunter (Scotland)
Steve Ison (England) †
Gerald Jackson (England)
Bob Kilby (England)
Sandor Levai (Hungary)
Wally Lloyd (England)
Les McGillivray (England)
Gordon McGregor (Scotland)
Doug McLauchlan (Australia)
Garry Middleton (Australia)
Ken Middleditch (England)
Tommy Miller (Scotland)
Paddy Mills (England)
Charlie Monk (Australia)
Geoff Mudge (Australia)
Charlie New (New Zealand)
Arne Pander (Denmark)
Ernie Price (England)
Bert Roger (England) +
Fred Rogers (England)
Tommy Roper (England)
Dick Seers (Australia)
Bruce Semmens (England)
Ken Sharples (England)
Bert Spencer (Australia)
Jimmy Squibb (England)
Tiger Stevenson (England)
Neil Street (Australia)
Roy Trigg (England)
Jack Unstead (England)
Peter Vandenberg (Australia)
Colin Watson (England)
Noel Watson (Australia) †
George Wilks (England)
Willie Wilson (Scotland)
Dave Younghusband (England)

†Norman Clay, Steve Ison and Noel Watson were talented young riders who were killed early in their careers, and would surely have qualified for world finals but for these tragic accidents.
*Malcolm Craven qualified as reserve in the cancelled 1939 final.
+Bert Roger actually qualified for the 1952 world final, but injury prevented him from riding.

George Wilks

Ray Duggan